To Dan
with warmest personal
regards.

NUTS COME IN PAIRS

All you wanted to know about couples' relationships and were afraid to ask!

NUTS COME IN PAIRS

All you wanted to know about couples' relationships and were afraid to ask!

Shepard D. Gellert

CITE PRESS, INC.
Huntington Station, NY

Printed in the United States of America

ISBN Number 0-9611122-0-4

Library of Congress Number 82-74154

Prologue

TEACH THE CHILDREN

A wise man
Who was asked about his parents
Once replied
"Of all the undertakings
God invented . . .
The parenthood career
Is the most important . . ."
Then he sighed
"How sad
That only amateurs
Attempt it!"

We must soon realize
That the happiness of man
Depends upon
His dear old Dad
And Mother
Who seldom understand
The love and care
A child demands
How could they
They don't understand each other!

Teach the children of the world
Teach them now before it gets too late
Teach them how to be the parents
Of tomorrow
Or they'll become the parents of today
And pass on all our hate and madness
To a whole new generation
And so it goes ad infinitum
Ad nauseum
Amen . . .

Words and music by Anthony Newley, and reprinted with his permission.

*I dedicate this book
to the children,
with the hope that they
will not have to go through the
needless suffering that we have experienced.*

Acknowledgments

I thank Madeleine Persoff for her many helpful and constructive suggestions in the preparation of the manuscript and for the long hours she devoted to editing and proofreading.

I am the director of the Redecision Institute, Center for Integrated Therapy and Education.

For many years the institute consisted of Grace Wilson, my co-therapist, and myself.

In the past ten years, over two thousand people passed through our doors, forming a community consisting of people who shared, cared, accepted, loved, and supported one another.

Some of the people in the community came to us—either to our workshops or into our supervisory groups—to train to be therapists or to improve their therapeutic skills. These we call trainees, and they range from board-certified psychiatrists, licensed psychologists, social workers, counselors, nuns, ministers, priests, business executives, teachers, to just plain folks. Some of these people we called staff: Tom Cox, Ted Jackson, Jan Miller, Rhonda Motyka, Mary Pandelaikis, Madeleine Persoff, and Lynn Slasor.

Some took graduate courses with me and became part of the community; these we call students.

Some, the largest segment, were those people who had been hurting and came to us to be healed. Those we call clients. They have made the most significant contribution to this book. They gave me the most love, the most support, the most acceptance— to them I am most deeply indebted. They understand why I dedicate this book to the children, rather than to them.

I am indebted to my parents, who did the best they could under extreme circumstances, and to the people over the years who have shown me love, affection, and kindness. I have always had difficulty in expressing appreciation, and I fear that outside of my awareness, I have treated some of those dear people shabbily. Life is a one-way journey; there is no roundtrip ticket. If I had the opportunity to do things over, I would do them differently. Several years ago, I saw a cartoon about mayflies, the larvae of a waterbug that hatch in May, live for twenty-four hours, mate, and die. One mayfly was saying to the other, "If only I knew nine hours ago what I know now." The joke is on us. This is the human condition.

I thank Dominic DiMattia, chairman of the Department of Counseling and Human Resources of the University of Bridgeport, for the opportunity to try out on an oppressed minority— the graduate student—and to refine much of the material contained in this book.

I acknowledge and thank the International Transactional Analysis Association and the *Journal of Transactional Analysis* for their permission to reprint and quote my own articles, sections of which are scattered throughout the book.

I also wish to thank Eileen Denker and Roberta Carey for their editorial help, and last, but by no means least, Don Hoak for his careful reading of the manuscript and for his very useful and helpful suggestions.

I may be criticized for not having sufficiently credited other workers in the field. My intentions have been to give a clear and precise presentation of facts and process and not to give a historical survey or bibliography of what has gone on before me. In defense, I quote Goethe."Kann und muss auch der Gelehrte seine Vorgaenger benutzen, ohne jedesman aengstlich anzudeuten, woher es ihm gekommen."*

Shepard D. Gellert

---

*"The scientist can and must use his forerunners (findings) without anxiously, each and every time, referring to his sources." Johann W. von Goethe, "Meteore des literarischen Himmels," in *Zur Naturwissenschaft im Allgemeinen (Plagiat)*. Cottasche Buchhandlung, Stuttgart, 1867, Vol. 35/36, p. 218.

Contents

NUTS COME IN PAIRS

All you wanted to know about couples' relationships and were afraid to ask!

CHAPTER 1

Introduction

We human beings are programmed on how to think, feel, and act by early life experiences; by our parents, our sisters and brothers, our uncles and aunts, our grandparents, our teachers, our peer group; and by happenings of fate—being bitten by a dog, being stung by a bee, being hit by a car, by childhood diseases, and by a shack falling on us.* Later in life we are not usually aware of our programming and think we are naturally stupid, smart, dumb, angry, bad, depressed, incapable, or superior.

Furthermore, we are creatures of intelligence and, outside of our awareness, can program ourselves and then use our abilities to stay happy or unhappy.

Hi, I'm Shepard Gellert. In this book I'll give examples of my own experiences, belief system, and interviews with clients for illustration. Many of us, with unerring accuracy, go through life getting ourselves kicked, dumped on, taken advantage of, put down, and persecuted. One of the major ways we keep ourselves miserable is by blaming others and trying to get others—society, our spouse, the environment—to change. At

---

*Shacks falling on us will be discussed in Chapter 2.

1

the same time we are blaming others, however, we are also creating many of the situations that make us miserable.

For example, a person who has been programmed to be angry will pick for a spouse someone who has been programmed to be depressed. Then if you ask him or her, "Why are you angry?" that person will answer, "I'm married to that sad sack who is withdrawn, doesn't meet my needs, won't talk to me," and so on. If you ask the spouse, "Why are you depressed?" he or she will tell you, "Of course I'm depressed. I'm coupled to that angry, hostile, critical S.O.B. all he (or she) does is put me down."

Consider Marge, who comes into therapy *thinking that she is unlovable*, suffering from low self-esteem, and *feeling rejected and sad. She acts cold and hostile* to members of the opposite sex.

Marge: I have a problem.

Shep: What's your problem?

Marge: My boyfriend is *always horny*. He is constantly after me. It's not safe in the car. He chases me in the kitchen; he has a one-track mind.

Shep: What do you think when your boyfriend is always horny?

Marge: *I think he doesn't love me. I feel rejected and sad and used.*

Shep: How do you act towards him?

Marge: *Cold and hostile.*

A year later Marge is back. She now has a new boyfriend.

Marge: I have a problem.

Shep: What's the problem?

Marge: *My boyfriend is never horny.* I have to make all the advances. As far as he is concerned, physical doesn't exist. The last time I heard him breathing hard, he was having an asthma attack.

Shep: What do you think when he is never horny?

Marge: *That he doesn't love me.*

Shep: What do you feel?

Marge: *Rejected and sad and used*; he is taking up my time, he eats like a horse, and I'm not getting any younger.

Shep: How do you behave?

Marge: *Cold and hostile.*

By blaming the situations, in this case on the boyfriends, Marge is able to maintain her old programming. Of course, Marge has to change her way of thinking, feeling, and acting. The *problem* is not in the environment. The problem is internal. We create most, if not all, of our personal problems.

Harry is similar to Marge, has low self-esteem, thinks he is unlovable, and is programmed to get himself rejected so he can feel miserable. Harry goes to a dance where there are 985 women, 984 of whom are lonely and looking to meet a man. With unerring accuracy he picks the 985th. He asks her to dance, and she tells him to "get lost." He leaves the dance feeling miserable, muttering to himself, "Why does this always happen to me?" and blaming his luck. His friend, Bad-breath, who looks like the hunchback of Notre Dame, walks out with two good looking women.*

Marvin spends the entire evening pursuing one woman sitting at a table with seven other women at a singles disco, only to find out at the end of the evening that she is getting married the next day and this is her "bachelorette party." Marvin walks out feeling angry.

In the preceding illustrations, any combination of feeling, thinking, or acting is possible. Even though we are all unique individuals, the process is the same. In each case the person could have felt hurt and angry, rejected and depressed, anxiety ridden and scared.

Our overall programming shows up in different patterns of thinking, feeling, and acting in various situations. Even though we may know better in specific situations, we behave in a manner that does not get us what we want. Later on, when the situation is past, we tell ourselves "I should have," "I could have," or "next time." When we sucessfully change patterns, even

---

*What's Badbreath's problem? With two women, his chances of developing a warm and loving relationship are not so hot. What are the women's problems? Badbreath's breath could knock down a fence post.

minor ones, we experience an increase in self-esteem, self-image, and self-confidence.

No school of therapy has all the answers. Today, there are many therapies. Some focus on changing your thinking, your behavior, your feelings, your body, what you eat, your relationships. Some don't focus on changing anything—objectively or subjectively visible. To some degree, most therapies are successful in producing change in their area of focus. The possible exception to this is orthodox Freudian psychoanalysis (the study of the id by the "odd").

I would like to illustrate several clinical cases where there was partial change.

Change of Acting and Self-Image

Samantha was thirty-five years old, single and *scared and tense*. Her family was nagging her about marriage. She had no boyfriends and would hassle with herself and worry about being an old maid. After five months of group therapy she reported she had a new problem: she was *scared and tense* because she had three boyfriends and was worried about which two to get rid of. Samantha had raised her self-esteem and changed her act (behavior), but not her pattern of hassling with herself; neither had she changed the way she felt. It was another year before she achieved her goals, felt good about herself, and had a monogamous relationship.

Change of Thinking

Ed was a complainer. He complained about his lousy job, his rotten customers, his rotten boss, the rotten government, ain't it awful what they're doing in Biafra—you name it. Complaints oozed from Ed. He would drive his family up a wall with his constant complaining. His major feeling was *anger*. After reading a couple of books on the power of positive thinking, Ed decided to change his thinking. He then became a model of acceptance of everything in the world.He changed his thinking, and became very *angry* at his family and drove them up the wall because they didn't share his rosy outlook on the universe. Ed thought he had made great changes through the power of positive thinking. But not so to his family, friends, and associates. It was not until his wife threatened him with divorce that he came into therapy and examined his programming of persecuting everyone.

Change of Feelings

Helen thought she was unlovable; she stayed *alone and withdrawn,* and felt scared when she was in her apartment. Her goal was not to feel scared when alone. After two months of therapy, she relived an early scene in which at the age of four she had been locked in a closet by her father as punishment, had heard fire engines outside, and thought the house was on fire and that she would be burned to death. She thought her parents had gone out and left her alone. After this experience, whenever she was alone, she would feel scared and did not know why.

After reliving the early scene in therapy, she no longer felt scared when she was alone in the house. She changed her feelings of fear, but not her thinking (self-image) or her acting: she was now comfortable staying *alone and withdrawn,* although she was not happy.

The neurotic is standing in a cesspool on tiptoe up to his neck in effluent. Too often what he/she gets in therapy is a telephone book so he/she can stand there comfortably, when all that's needed is courage to get out of the cesspool.

It is my hope that this book will help people avoid the mistakes I have made by blaming everyone and everything, except myself, for my mistakes.

CHAPTER 2

Why?

People are always asking me, "why?"

The answer to the question, "Why are we programmed?" properly belongs in the realm of speculative philosophy, rather than in the realm of psychology or personality theory.*

When I am lecturing, I am often asked the question, "Why is it that my cousin Tom, from Omaha, does such and such and so and so?" My answer to this question of "why" is, "*because a shack fell on him.*" Implied in the question is that an authority figure should know "why," given enough data, and this is just not true. The authority can no more answer the "why" than he or she can give an explanation for *why* God made little green apples.

Consider six little five-year-old kids playing in a shack: Tom, Dick, Harry, Jill, Judy, and Dotty. The shack collapses on them, and they are almost suffocated. However, people passing by dig them out in time.

Little Tom is back in school the next week, where he is confronted by the teacher and principal for smashing a window. He

*Sandor Rado, Freud's disciple, founder of the New York Psychoanalytic Institute and the "Typhoid Mary" of psychoanalysis in the United States, wrote in the early 1930s, "In psychoanalysis, the 'why' has swallowed the 'how'."

feels as if they're closing in on him, and he begins to stutter. Now Tom is forty-six years old, and he still stutters. Why does Tom stutter when faced with authority figures? *Answer:* Because a shack fell on him when he was five years old.

Little Dick goes home. Because of his experience, his mother is terrified lest he get hurt, so she keeps him at home and is very careful about whom he plays with, what he does, and where he is. She doesn't let him out of her sight. Forty years later Dick is a bachelor, lives with his mother, and doesn't have many friends. Why is Dick a momma's boy? *Answer:* Because a shack fell on him when he was five years old.

Little Harry goes home, and his father beats the tar out of him because he tore his pants. Little Harry thinks to himself: "They'll be sorry some day when I'm dead."* At the age of nineteen Harry is killed in a motorcycle accident. Why did Harry die so young? *Answer:* Because a shack fell on him when he was five years old.

Little Jill goes home and tells her parents all about her experience, and her father *beams* at her and says, "My little girl is one tough fighter." Forty years later Jill is vice-president of an advertising agency in a position where infighting counts in a highly competitive situation. Why is Jill the vice-president? *Answer:* Because a shack fell on her.

Little Judy goes home, and her parents are worried about her. But since they both work, they make Theresa, her older sister, take care of her. Theresa now has to take Judy with her whenever she goes out to play. She has to stay home and help Judy, and is really angry about this. Forty years later Theresa is very angry; she is taking care of her family, her husband, her children, the world in general, but not taking care of herself. Judy now lives two thousand miles from her sister. Judy is helpless, "can't" do things, and is dependent on her husband to make decisions and take care of her. He is angry and feels like a martyr. Why is Judy helpless, resentful, and depressed? Why is Judy's husband angry? And why is Judy's sister, Theresa, such a caretaker and so angry? *Answer:* Because a shack fell on Judy when she was five years old.

*Very common in people with depression is the childhood thought "they'll be sorry when I'm dead" or some variation.

Little Dotty goes home to her parents. Her mother is very strong and aggressive; her father is very weak and passive. Up until this time, they have given Dotty a lot of recognition for being a tomboy. They always wanted a boy, anyway. When she comes home, her father looks at her approvingly and says, "Boy, you are tough." Little Dotty hears (1) she is a boy, and (2) she is tough. Forty years later, Dotty is working on a construction site and tough. Why is Dotty tough? *Answer:* Because a shack fell on her when she was a little girl.

All these examples illustrate that the historical approach is extremely unsatisfactory for answering "why" questions.

In my experience, people do not change until they stop asking *"Why* am I this way?" and start asking "How can I *change?"* Now that I have more or less demolished the question "why," I will attempt to answer it with my own thinking. This is pure speculation, so feel free to disagree.

Consider a baby girl turtle inside an egg buried in a sand dune. She breaks through the egg shell and runs into the ocean. Meanwhile, the frigate birds are swooping down, eating little turtles. If she makes it into the ocean, she swims three thousand miles to some specific area of the ocean, gains thirty or forty pounds in the next ten years, swims back to the exact same beach, digs a hole, lays eggs, and goes back into the ocean. The little turtle has complete genetic* programming. We label this *instinct.* She knows what to eat, how to catch fish, how to properly estimate the distance from the fish to her mouth, and so forth. And she has a full set of drives for survival of herself and the species.

The turtle is not adaptable. If there is a log in her way, she may not make it to the ocean. She doesn't know, and is unable to figure out, alternative behavior patterns. If the beach is polluted, the turtle will disappear as a species. She does have memory, but it is extremely limited.

---

*Now that I have the label, I can think I really know something; that is, genetic material carries species memory, ontology precedes phylogeny, cha, cha, cha. I can sound learned, even erudite, but I still don't know doodly do. If you like, you can substitue "God-given" for "genetic" wherever genetic appears in this book and the meaning won't change. About 20 percent of this book is pure bull and 80 percent pure truth. Unfortunately, I don't know which 20 percent is bull. The reader will have to decide. I figure this is a big improvement over most of the books in the field, which run between 50 percent and 98 percent bull.

People, on the other hand, are highly adaptable. The human being as a species has spread over the face of the earth—in the jungles of the equatorial belt, in the plains of the temperate zones, and in the frigid Arctic circles. At birth an infant has genetic programming, just as the little turtle has. The infant knows how to suck, how to cry, is capable of programming muscular movements, and has all the drives and instincts of survival of the self and the species. What makes people so adaptable is that they are capable of *secondary programming after birth*. To restate this, the human as a species is capable of remembering experience, using experience, and passing learned messages and programming from one generation to another. This is a major difference between turtles and people as species. People develop a mind capable of logic and secondary programming, which we call *parenting*.

In primitive tribes today, such as those who live in the Amazon and in Borneo, the secondary programming does not change very much, if at all, from generation to generation; nor did it change in humans a few thousand years ago. Climactic conditions change very slowly. Three-year-olds in primitive culture are capable of taking care of themselves.* They know which animals and poisonous snakes to avoid, how to avoid sharp tools and fire. They will not go near a ledge where there's a steep drop and are fully capable of building nets and catching birds. Should they be separated from their parents, they would have some chance of survival.

Not so in today's Western culture. We are not programmed at the age of three to know that a car can hit us, or how to open a can of beans. Our culture and technological development has changed enormously in the past thousand years. For example, one hundred years ago in the United States, four- and five-year-old children were working ten to fourteen hours a day in mines and factories. Now I see forty-year old adolescents "working" on their PhD's.

The two main genetic directives, survival of the species and survival of the self, include programming for happiness! Our genetic inheritance—the capacity for joy, creativity, intuition, a

---

*Heinz Werner, *Comparative Psychology of Mental Development*, International University Press, N.Y., 1945.

keen sense of awareness of touch, smell, hearing, intimacy, and love—have been overridden by our secondary programming in the interests of survival in today's complex culture.

In our own society and culture, the child is programmed not to be himself or herself: "Don't be you." A little boy runs into the street and his parents are scared. So they give him a whack on the rear end and tell him not to run into the street. Now they've transferred the hot potato, and the little kid is scared instead of the parents being scared. Once the kid is scared, the parents can relax. It is very important that small children be taught not to run into the street, for survival. There is no "good" way to do this. One cannot reason with two-year-olds. They do not have the brain capacity for abstract thinking. An unfortunate but necessary message is, "Don't do what it is you want to do," or "Don't be you." Little kids go into the supermarket and want to pull out the bottom can of a pyramid of canned peas. The mother says, "That's not nice. Behave yourself. Don't do that." Unfortunately, this is a necessary "don't be you" message! If we were three-years-old and lived in the jungle, we would instinctively know how to stay away from the snakes, lions, and tigers. This is not true in today's corporate jungle, Times Square, the single's scene, or Central Park.

All this is written through the distortion of Western culture. However, even climate affects programming. Studies indicate that Eskimo parents, whose children spend little time outside playing, do not display high levels of emotion and discipline children verbally; in African tribes, on the other hand, in which the people spend a great deal of their time outdoors, parents use violence and yell and scream, displaying high emotional levels. One research attributes these behaviours to the fact that in the warm climates the kids can get away and run from their parents till their parents cool off. In an igloo full of little Eskimos, however, the noise level and expenditure of energy would be intolerable. Different cultures, different programming! Furthermore, this entire book is written through the distortions of my own patterning and personal background.

"Why is it that my cousin, Tom, from Omaha, does such and such and so and so?" I have already explained it's because a shack fell on him, but that is not the whole "truth." Tom does such and such and so and so because he was born an infant!

At birth an infant has a very primitive brain. Only after three years do the prefrontal regions of the cortex reach the stage of cell development that the motor regions have already attained at eleven months!

The thought processes of young children are extremely concrete, so that they hear the *literal meaning* of what is said, not what their parents think they said. That part of the brain used in child thought processes is extremely intuitive, creative, and spontaneous, and the little child constantly scans adults and parents to sense what they are saying nonverbally.

If the father says in an angry voice, "Don't let me catch you doing that again," the child hears, "Do it again, but don't get caught." The child feels scared. He or she will do it again, feel scared, and try not to get caught. Later in life people will feel guilty when they do what their parents would not approve of.

The parent says, "Try to keep your room neat," and the child hears an instruction, "Don't keep your room neat, just try to." "Try" in this case equals "don't."

The parent says, "Why don't you keep your room neat?" and the child hears, "Tell me why you don't keep your room neat," and will proceed to give an answer with a historical "because."

The parent says, "This won't hurt." Little children are far more sensitive to pain than are grownups, and they translate what was said into, "Get ready for thirty stitches without anesthesia."

The parent says, "Don't stick beans in your ears." There will be lots of excitement in this house.

A four-year-old hears "Make up your mind to keep your room neat" as "You have an unmade mind, whatever that is, (like an unmade bed), but whatever it is you're not okay."

"Don't act childish" (to a four-year-old who doesn't know what "childish" is) means "Something's wrong with you."

After the age of five our brain cells are first fully developed in the cerebral cortex,* and we begin to develop selective per-

*Karl Pribram, *Languages of the Brain*, Prentice Hall, Englewood Cliffs, N.J., 1971.

ception and concrete logic. By age eighteen we have maximum cell development in the prefrontal cortex, and we block out vast quantities of data. Even as you read this book, you are blocking out sounds of the street, body awareness; if you are really engrossed, dinner may be burning in the oven. This blocking out of vast quantities of data is called selective perception. If you smell smoke or if the telephone rings, you immediately become alert to handling these interruptions, whereas if the kids make noise or a canon goes off in the next room, that may not bother you.

In later life we will not be in touch with what is going on in the younger part of ourselves. We develop childhood amnesia. To some degree in all of us, the abstract thinking part, the part we are in touch with, is cut off from what is going on in the rest of us. Primitive man had to be constantly in touch with his senses for survival in the jungle. Not so in our present culture.

Very early childhood memories are not usually available to our consciousness, but they are intact, influencing every aspect of our entire lives, and they can be demonstrated with the aid of electric brain stimulation, deep hypnosis, or relaxation techniques.

By the time my son was four years old, he had been watching his sister go to school for a year. On the days she didn't go to school she wore blue jeans, as he did. On the days she did go to school, she wore a dress. He, too, wanted to go to school. One day he told his mother in a sorrowful voice, "I wanna put on a dress like Hootie (he couldn't pronounce Susie) and go to school." He identified going to school with wearing a dress, and he had not distinguished between boys wearing pants and girls wearing dresses.

When I was five or six, Mom trained me to be sneaky. She would buy a box of candy, give me one piece, and then hide the box. She would say, "Don't eat the candy. It's for company" (which never came). This was like telling a ravenous cat in a fish market not to eat fish. The first chance I got I would initiate a search-and-destroy operation, find the box of candy, and take two pieces. The next day I would think and do the same thing. Two days later, repeat performance. Three days later, repeat performance. Within a week or so, all that was left in the box were three jellies, which I didn't like. After about a month, Mom would remove the box and much to her "surprise" she would find that I had eaten all the candy. Had mom been straight, she would have left the candy out and told me not to take any! She would call me and ask, "Did you do this?" Who else would have done it? I would sheepishly admit, "Yes," and then I would not be punished. I remember thinking: "How did she know that I did it?" Mom was not aware that she was training me to be sneaky. If asked, she probably would have said, "I am teaching Buddy to be honest." Incidentally, I am told that my grandmother used to do the same thing with chocolate bars, and my grandfather (Mom's side), who died before I was born, always had candy in his breast pocket so that the kids could "steal" it. It's not hard to see where Mom learned this little game.

A major problem in training psychotherapists is that they often forget that the young child does not think or perceive the way adults do, and that *all* of us, when we are feeling an emotion, are to some degree incapable of abstract symbolic, logical thinking and respond from our child part.

If intelligence and thinking could cure us or make us happy, we would all be the epitome of mental health and joy. As a species, we are not stupid.

I have given some examples of "why"; the remainder of this book focuses on "how" we are programmed and "how" to increase our options so that we don't spend the rest of our lives diving into cesspools, running into stone walls, and trying to push doors out that are hinged to open inward (and vice versa).

If after reading this book you are not satisfied, your misery will be cheerfully refunded.

CHAPTER 3

How We Are Programmed Through Recognition

Negative Recognition or Strokes

The rat psychologists* explain things simply. They construct a Y-shaped box with one passageway leading to little rats' paradise and the other passageway leading to a dark, dank, and icky box. In the passage of the Y that goes to rats' paradise they install an electric shock. Little rats, being fun- and joy-loving creatures, when placed in the Y immediately make for little rats' paradise, and wham!, they get a shock. They then run into the box, where they cower in terror and feel bad. After thirty or forty mild shocks or five or ten severe shocks that almost kill a little rat, or maybe a mix of twenty mild and two severe shocks, it stays out of the path that leads to paradise and runs straight into the black, icky box. After the little rat has been programmed, the rat psychologist substitutes a buzzer for the shocker. Little rats have a short memory, and every forty days or so they may forget and make for paradise. When they do, they hear the buzz and run back into the box. Thirty, forty or fifty rat years later

---

*Experimental psychologists, unlike other psychologists, psychotherapists, psychiatrists, and psychoanalysts, follow the scientific method and make less money. Naturally, their work and findings are ignored to a great degree by the other "professionals" in the field.

we have a big, powerful rat who stays cowering in the icky box the rest of its life and suffers. It has been patterned by early life experiences and remains unaware that this suffering is optional.

We are far more complex than little rats, although quite a few of us have (had) parents who use(d) the equivalent of electric shocks and buzzers on us. Most parents love their children and want the best for them, but outside their awareness, they were programmed by *their* parents, who were programmed by *their* parents, who were programmed by *their* parents, that this is *the way* to raise children.

Studies have shown that infants need physical touching, or they will develop "hospital disease" or marasmus* and either die or grow up badly damaged emotionally and mentally.

When we get older, we *substitute* the need for physical stroking with other forms of recognition, such as verbal compliments or put-downs, a paycheck, promotion, or election as club president. Infants learn very quickly what to do to get recognition (strokes). It is a matter of survival, so infants do not distinguish between pleasure and pain. A kiss or a kick has the same survival value. To infants, stroking is as necessary as oxygen, so it's as though young children are wearing an oxygen mask, with the parents and other parent figures controlling the valve.

If infants are "good" but do not receive enough stroking (recognition), they quickly learn what to do to get their parents to come in and give them attention. If they can't get positive strokes by being "good", they will do something that upsets their parents so that the parents will give them negative strokes. Later in life, these children will grow up to become what is known as "kick me" players, going through life *wanting positive strokes* but setting things up so that they get kicked instead of kissed; that is, they get negative recognition instead of positive recognition. Negative recognition is better than no recognition at all, just as bad breath is better than no breath, and high-blood pressure is better than no blood pressure, but negative recognition isn't conducive to happiness.

If children are programmed to seek negative recognition, then negative recognition reinforces the undesired behavior!

*Rene Spitz, "Hospitalism, Genesis of Psychiatric Conditions in Early Childhood," *Psychoanalytic Study of the Child*, I (1945), pp. 53—74.

Positive Recognition or Strokes

There is another way to program little rats—by positive reinforcement, something the little rat needs or wants is offered as a reward. In positive reinforcement, the rat psychologist puts the rat into a maze with a right and a wrong way, or into a cage where there are two levers, a right lever and a wrong lever. When the little rat enters the right branch of the maze or pushes the correct lever, it gets a reward, like a food pellet.

For us human beings positive conditional recognition is: I love you when you behave yourself, are good, study hard, take out the garbage, do what I say, don't ask for attention, get lost, don't yell and scream, don't jump and don't be happy. We can also be programmed to get positive conditional strokes through negative behavior. I have worked with children who were "spoiled rotten" and with clients who, when they were children, were spoiled rotten. They were not spoiled rotten by an overabundance of positive *unconditional* stroking. The usual case was that their parents trained them to get their way by acting out; that is, if they had a temper tantrum, they got the toy, and no strokes when they "behaved." Of course, their parents could have let them have the temper tantrum and not responded. There are options. Positive unconditional recognition is: I love you for you, without conditions.

If the child gets enough positive *unconditional* strokes, chances are that he or she will not be affected by any heavy conditioning given through positive *conditional* strokes. If the child is starved for recognition, then the rare positive stroke, conditional or unconditional, will have great effect. Some of us are alive and sane today because of some minor positive stroking from a parental figure, a teacher, a neighbor, a minister, or a relative.

Although I imagine it is theoretically possible to program a child by solely positive conditional stroking, I have yet to see the case where this was the situation. I have yet to meet parents who tell me that they hide and wait to catch their children doing something good and then run out and give positive strokes! I have yet to meet a client who has said that he or she used to tingle with joy and anticipation when his or her mother would say "Wait until your father gets home and I tell him about the good things you did today and have him take you to the circus." This population may well exist, but it doesn't show up in the therapist's office.

The Power of the Positive Stroke

Joey, the youngest of four boys, at fifty, won the nomination from his political party for judgeship. He had always felt he was a failure, because all the older brothers were wealthy and had "made it big." He and a brother went to visit their eighty-four-year-old mother in a nursing home. His brother enthusiastically told her, "Joey has won the nomination from the party for judge." The mother looked at Joey and said, "So what's better, a judge or a doctor?" Joey never got positive recognition as a child. His entire life had been one disaster after another in his personal relationships. He would fall in love with any woman who was kind or considerate. The smallest positive recognition from a woman, and he would act like a teenager with a crush on his first date. He was so starved for positive recognition that when he did get some positive recognition, the "he" would disappear. There was no "he." He was like a lonely puppy and would smother the women he dated with gifts, phone calls, attention, not letting them breathe. Women, of course, want a man, not a puppy; and after the infatuation wore off for them, they would drop him.

When people come to me straight from a break-up in a relationship or from a divorce, I warn them, especially those with low self-esteem, not to confuse kindness or consideration or sex with love. From the point of view of the giver of the recognition, it can be extremely uncomfortable to have someone fall in love with the giver because he or she was kind, considerate, or horny.

Based on our own subjective, early childhood experiences and the level of intensity of positive/negative recognition as we were growing up, we all have our own individual internal perception, and we are likely to perceive other people quite differently and distort the message they are sending.

In a household in which the parents usually scold in a quiet voice, yelling would have an impact.

In a household in which the parents usually yell, the child adapts and thinks this is the way the world is, and a slap will have an impact.

If the norm is to get slapped for the slightest infraction of whatever the parents consider good, nice, then what will happen is that this mild slap will be considered the norm, and the child will go ahead with his or her behavior. If the child needs negative attention, he or she will do something and get the mild slap. Punishment to this child will be the occasional beating with the strap.

If the strap is the norm, then the child adapts to this. "Doesn't everyone get beaten with a strap for making noise?" Then something else, one of the horrors we read about in the newpaper, will come to mean punishment to the child.

Human beings however, often give nonverbal messages they are not aware of. We may think we are being very friendly, while nonverbally radiating hostility. We can also give mixed verbal messages at the same time we are giving a congruent or noncongruent nonverbal message.

Mixed Verbal Recognition

An unconditional positive stroke is "I love you"—in transactional analysis jargon, a "warm fuzzie." A "cold pricklie," on the other hand, is a straight negative stroke, unconditional—"I hate you. Get lost." If we crossbreed warm fuzzies and cold pricklies, we get warm pricklies and cold fuzzies.

When we get a warm pricklie, it feels good. For example, I love Joe and Joe loves me, and we are delighted to meet each other on the street, but since men don't express affection in our culture, when I see Joe I say, "Hello Joe, you old SOB," radiating warmth, and Joe will look at me, radiating warmth, and say, "Shep, you old bastard, how are you?" We then part and I feel good and Joe feels good. Warm pricklies *feel good*. The reality was that I called him an "SOB" and he called me a "bastard"; worse yet, he called me an *old* bastard.

When we get a *cold fuzzie*, on the other hand, we walk away shaking our head, as if somebody slashed our back with a razor. We know we should think we've been complimented, but we feel cold. For example, "You surprise me how fast you catch on." The not-so-secret message is, "You're stupid." "I like the way you look today" (emphasis on the today), meaning "usually you don't look so good."

"You look good—who's your embalmer?" "I just adore that dress. Of course, it isn't my taste." Girl to boy "Gee, you're light on your feet," meaning, "I'm surprised that you, an overgrown ox, haven't totally smashed every bone in my foot." Boy to girl, thinking he is giving her a compliment, "Gee, that dance was great. You don't sweat much for a fat girl." Then the boy will wonder why she doesn't go out with him.

A forty-year-old client came to me for therapy in the middle of a divorce. She absolutely could not give positive strokes. Although the norm in our group therapy is to come in and hug me in the beginning of each session, she would not hug me. After about the eighth week, I knew she loved me because she would come in and hit me on the arm. She had bony little fists, and it really hurt. However, I didn't say, "Hey, your're hitting me, it hurts." For her, making contact was a big thing and meant she felt free to touch me. After about four months of therapy, she stopped hitting me and began giving me a very, very light, short hug. After another two or three months, she would give a very short hug. At this time, she started to date. She is very happily married today to a warm and loving person.

When I was about nine years old, if you liked a girl, you would either punch her, hit her, dip her pigtails in the inkwell, or throw spitballs in her hair. Many grown-ups never mature out of this stage and express love to children by pinching them, poking them, teasing them verbally, or otherwise tormenting them.

We need to increase our awareness and the awareness of others on how programming can be changed through the use of positive stokes.

CHAPTER 4

Early Messages

When I was growing up, I was punished for the little things I did. Usually the punishment was a beating from my father, and I went through life being afraid of him, for good reason: I was programmed by my mother to do these things to get him to beat me, and then I would get one tenth of a positive stroke of approval from her for having gotten my father to blow his stack. It showed the world what a beast he was and how she suffered.

When I did something really "bad," I wasn't physically punished. When I was four years old, I was visiting my Uncle Max in East Orange, New Jersey. In those days that was "out in the country." Two five- and six-year-old girls, a major's daughters, lived nearby. They told me that if I let them watch me "wee-wee", they would let me watch them "wee-wee." I agreed. I knew boys were different from girls, but didn't know how. I wee-weed and they watched, then they ran away. When they met me, the next day they pulled the same con, but by now I was wise. I said, "You first." They said, "No, you first." So I went up on top of a big rock and stood up over them, took it out, and wee-weed all over them. I thought I was brilliant. They ran home and told their mother, who told my uncle, who told my mother. When I went for lunch, the atmosphere was so heavy you could have cut it with a knife. I got sent to my room, but *I didn't get beaten*! I was never asked or allowed to tell my side of the story.

If I did minor things such as lose my hat, tear my clothes, break my glasses, I got punished. At East Orange that same summer, my Uncle Lionel, a Freudian psychiatrist who hated children, had a model-A Ford with a rumble seat, which he had painted black. The apple of his eye. I got into the garage and found some orange and green paint and repainted his fenders. I knew I had committed a terrible crime when they hid me from Uncle Lionel until he left, but I did not get punished.

When I was about ten years old another kid and I took a heavy steel wire we had found and tied it from a fire hydrant to a telephone pole across the street. A car came along and the wire wrapped around the axle. We ran away, of course. I didn't know it, but my father had just come home and had seen the whole incident. Looking back, maybe I did have a sixth sense that he would be coming home. In any event, he crawled under the car and it took him forty-five minutes to get the axle free. He went home filthy and was washing up when I arrived home. The second I walked in the door, I knew something was wrong. My mother said, "Go to your room, take a bath, and then go to bed." I was not physically punished.

The slightest remark, the smallest thing would trigger a beating. The absence of punishment for heavy "misdeeds" was the equivalent of positive recognition or reinforcement. Outside their awareness, one of the ways our parents train us to be spoiled, sneaky, rebellious, compliant is through the stroke economy (positive and negative recognition), just as they were trained, and just as we train our children how to think, feel, and act.

Parents do not deliberately program their children to suffer. It is done outside their awareness. At the time, they may or may not be aware of how they are behaving or feeling! Parents' nonverbal behavior is far more powerful than their verbal. Unfortunately, countless people have spent years in therapy talking about what their parents said, rather than what they did!

A perfect example from scripture is *Proverbs*, Solomon's advice to his sons. Solomon ranted and raved against sexual depravity. That's what he said! What he did is another story: he blew a fortune on women and on the temple (conspicuous consumption), had his own private army, and broke more commandments than you could shake a stick at. He got away with it, and that's why he was reknown for his "wisdom." As Solomon's nonverbal messages carried more weight than his verbal messages in the programming of his children, so do ours. You may recognize some of the following as messages you have received or given.

"Be Perfect"

One of the most common messages and patterning parents give their children is "be perfect." A little kid comes home from school and says, "I got a 90", and Mom or Dad says, "That's nice. Try harder." He then comes home and says, "I got a 95." They tell him, "Study some more" or "What happened to the other 5 points?" He then comes home and says, "I got 100." The parents say, "It must have been an easy test" or "Maybe now you can start to work on your behavior, penmanship, cleaning up your room, or. . ." No matter what the child does, it's not good enough.

The secret message depends on whether or not you have been programmed to be compliant or rebellious (defiant). If you are programmed to be defiant or rebellious, the secret message is *don't make it*! When you make it, you don't get recognition or get minor recognition, but if you fail, you get massive recognition.

If you are programmed to be compliant, the secret message is *work hard and don't enjoy it*. If you have developed as a hypercritical person, you will work hard and not enjoy it. No matter what you do, it's not good enough because you can never be perfect; so you'll never be satisfied with yourself. Furthermore, you may never be satisfied with what someone else (for example, your spouse or your children) does! Either way it's no good, and people with a "be perfect" message will go through life hassling themselves. The underlying dynamics are that the parents are scared that the child won't make it. Because they're scared, they never give the child recognition to any degree for making it, only recognition for not making it, and *negative recognition reinforces the undesired behavior*. Furthermore, the parents will role-model the undesired behavior, so if you have a "don't make it" message, either the mother or the father will be in the business of not making it in some area of life: social, personal, or financial. If you have a "work hard" and "don't enjoy it" parent message, then your mother or your father is in the same business to show you how.

"Don't Belong"

A less common message is "don't belong." If people have a "don't belong" message, no matter where they are, they *feel* as if they don't belong. Very often this is accompanied by a dual feeling of superiority/inferiority. In a social setting they feel superior to other people because the others are not brilliant, they don't know how to dress, they don't have as much money as you do, or they're not as familiar with the classics. At the same time they feel inferior because the others are having a good time, are being intimate and loving, and are having fun, and they are not.

A client, aged twenty, came in for counseling because he felt that no matter where he was, he didn't belong. His father came to the United States as a young man and moved to a small town where he was the only one who spoke broken English. The father felt that he never belonged and wanted to spare his son the misery he had gone through. As a result he made his son dress for school every day wearing a shirt and a tie, which he felt would help him be accepted. The father was very strict; the client had to come home directly from school and study so he would make it. As a result the client never played with other kids, was a straight A scholar, and at the age of twenty had a PhD in mathematics. The father was scared that the son wouldn't belong and was hypercritical and controlling. What he feared most was what he had produced in his son. The son was completely lacking in social skills. He didn't know how to talk to girls, was shy and withdrawn, and felt as if he didn't belong.

There is no cookbook of "secret messages"; it depends on the total family patterning, and the above cases are to illustrate the process. One client was programmed to be compliant. His younger brother, he told me, was a high school truant, who hung out with a bunch of teenagers who were stealing cars and smoking pot. It is easy to see that the younger brother is *rebellious*, not conforming to society's rules, but I suspect he also bought the secret message, "don't belong."

The rebellious child with the "don't belong" message will seek a peer group of "don't belongers," the worst kids in school, later a lunatic fringe group of some type. Rebellious children follow the secret message, but in their awareness, they think they are doing the opposite of what their parents are saying!

The oddest *don't belong* I've ever come across was a client who said she never felt that she was part of anything. I asked her what her birth story was. She said her mother always told her she was *something special* because she had been born in a *whale*, and growing up she believed she had been born in a *whale*. She considered herself somehow different from other children, but when she was eight years old she found out that she was not born in a whale, she had been born in a veil, a thin membrane covering the infant's face. Among the old-country Jews two generations ago, a child being born in a veil was considered a lucky occurrence, something special, like the seventh son of the seventh son. Her mother had a heavy Jewish accent, pronounced *W*'s like *V*'s and pronounced *veil* as *vay-ull*. The young part of the client believed she was born in a whale and was "something special," even though the older part knew better.

"Don't Be Well"

My mother was a very cold woman. However, I'm sure she loved me very much and was terrified lest I be a failure like my father, so most of the time she nagged me about (you name it). My father was very depressed, usually ignored me, criticized me, or disciplined me. At rare times, he would be close to me and take me fishing, ice skating, roller skating, or bicycle riding. When I was sick, my mother would not nag and my father was warm and gentle and kind and loving.

This patterning for me went back to infancy. As an infant I had double pneumonia, and although I have no recall, I'm sure I had a lot of tender, loving care. All through childhood I suffered through colds, earaches, and ear abscesses. I distinctly remember the concern and care shown me by both my parents when I had whooping cough and a mastoidectomy from which I almost died. The nonverbal message was, "As long as you are sick, we'll love you. If you're not sick, then we'll worry about you and be scared that you're not going to make it, and be on your case twenty-four hours a day."

I went into the army at the age of seventeen, and my mother's great concern was I would have colds. I spent four years in the army, sleeping on the ground in all kinds of weather, and had about two colds and one earache. Since getting in touch with this programming, I seldom have a cold.

It boils down to massive stroking and tender, loving care if children are sick, and negative stroking or no stroking if they are well. I have had clients who trained their children to be sick; at the slightest sniffle, they drag them to the doctor. Lots of attention to illness. The secret message *for me* was be dependent, and when I was sick or had *problems*, my parents would rescue me.

"Don't Grow Up/Don't Be a Child"

Usually* the oldest one in the family is envious of the younger ones. He or she wants to go on the carousel ride or play in the sandbox; however, the parents say, "Don't be a child. You're too big for that." The younger ones are envious of the older ones, so at the age of four, they want to go to school and stay up late, but are too young: "Oh, you're too little for that," which is a "don't grow up" message. One child may be told "don't be a child" and the other one "don't grow up." The oldest one gets positive strokes for not being a child and negative strokes when he or she is a child. The younger ones get positive recognition for being children or dependent, and no recognition or negative recognition when they grow up and do for themselves. It's expected.

In a couple's relationship, very often one partner has the "don't grow up" message, and the other partner has the "don't be a child" one. Historically, "don't be a child" and "be in-

---

*"Usually" means that exceptions are fairly common!

dependent'' were probably the major messages. A few generations ago the oldest one would certainly catch the ''don't be a child,'' because he or she would be needed to take care of the family. The ''don't grow up'' message is probably a cultural effect due to affluence. In my father's time, most children got ''don't be a child.'' School was let out during harvest time so that the children could work. If there is a major secret message in ''don't grow up,'' it is ''be dependent.'' ''Be dependent'' will be reinforced in many different ways with other messages, verbal and nonverbal. People who go crazy and get themselves hospitalized are in effect following a ''be dependent'' message, being dependent on parents or society. One of the ways they can remain dependent is by going bonkers. More common are the persons who are programmed to think they are going crazy.

"Be Scared of Going Crazy"

Crazy people usually think they are sane, so if you *think* you are crazy, you're probably really sane.

Any time Virginia was happy or excited or exhibiting childlike behavior when she was young, her mother would scold her, ''That's crazy.'' The overt message was ''don't feel happy'' and ''don't be a child.'' She came into group therapy because she was isolated, had no friends, was almost a recluse, and every time she felt happy, *she thought* she was going crazy. She was a school teacher. In group therapy one night she said, ''Today the kids were acting real crazy, and I was terrified.'' I asked her to show me by acting out the children's crazy behavior. What she acted for me normal behavior of children—horsing around, making faces at each other, laughing, giggling. She identified this as crazy behavior. I asked her when she most often felt that she was going crazy, and she described social situations in which people were happy. The group gave her feedback that feeling happy is not going crazy, and it is okay to feel happy. That one evening changed her whole life. She was able to make friends, be happy, and when last heard from, she was engaged to be married. I never determined the secret message, but I suspect it was ''stay single so you can take care of me,'' since she was a caretaker and was staying single.

"Don't Feel"

A child may be told "You're not tired, you're angry," or "You're not angry, you're tired,"—Either message is almost a direct message to feel depressed. Little children do not feel the way grownups feel. They feel all or nothing. When the infant's tummy is full, he or she feels infantile euphoria. If the tummy is empty, he or she feels the black hole despair—nothingness, pure misery, and terror. Parents tell the child, "You're very brave. You don't feel anything," or (my mother talking to Aunt Stella), "Buddy is so good. He sits in the dentist's chair and there isn't a peep out of him!" This is an attribution: "don't feel."

Some of us develop extremely high thresholds of pain: We come home with a compound fracture and are told "that's nothing." Others of us are extremely sensitive to physical pain: The slightest scrape and our parents make a big fuss and tell us it must be very painful. The more experience I get, the less I believe in individual hereditary differences, although they do exist.

Of course, no parents tell their children, "don't be well," "don't be happy," "be perfect," "don't feel." These are artificial abstractions and classifications, products of a total configuration of a family system we grew up in.

Now that we've seen some examples of secret messages, I'd like to focus attention on the process involved.

The process is identical in all illustrations. In the "be perfect" message, both parents are usually hypercritical. If you are programmed to be hypercritical, you can turn it in on yourself or you can turn it out on others. A hypercritical person, who can spot a fly speck on a whitewashed wall at ten thousand yards, can see blemishes in everyone. This way he or she can go through life faulting everybody, seeing what's wrong with everybody, and not seeing what's wrong with himself or herself. Or else he or she sees that everybody is much better than he or she is, and constantly puts himself or herself down.

In my case, I spent forty-six years being hypercritical, missing the joy of life and acceptance of others. What I wanted most was to be loved and accepted; what I set up, outside my awareness, was for people to flee from me because of my own criticality.

A lesson can be learned in this. What I *fear* the most is what I cause to happen, and what I *want* the most is what I stop myself from getting. This may sound ridiculous on the surface, but examine it. If what I want most is for my son to make it, then what I'm doing outside my awareness is stopping him. What I fear most, that my son will have a "don't make it" message, is what I'm producing by being hypercritical of him, by giving him a "be perfect" message.

A common pattern with children who are either dyslexic or have a physical impairment is that the parents' greatest *fear* is that the kid will grow up and *will not be independent*. Often outside their awareness, they do everything for the child, constantly helping and therefore programming him or her to be helpless and dependent.

In doing family therapy, working with children as well as their parents, I have seen this situation over and over again. If the parents lead miserable lives and suffer, what they want most is that their children be happy. Outside their awareness they model suffering.

Nonverbal messages come through the modeling of parents, siblings, the peer group, and the culture. This is so universal as to be overlooked. Time messages are often given through the nonverbal modeling of parents, so if the father dies at the age of fifty-two, a person who has a "don't be better than your father" message may experience anxiety or depression at the age of fifty-two. If the father was successful in business for ten years and then neglected business and became a drunk, the son may also follow the father's pattern.

If you are a parent, it is very important that you do not blame yourself and that you do not blame your parents for what they "have done to you." The important thing is to change, not blame.

When I was little, sex in our house was absolutely, positively forbidden. My mother never would kid around and joke about sex; when my uncles came over and told a risque or off-color story, she would not smile, not laugh; her attitude was that it was disgusting. This attitude was reinforced when I was older in many, many different ways. I recall her telling my sister it was all right not to get married. She could grow up and be a school teacher, and if she did get married, she shouldn't have children.

My father's attitude toward sex was also atrocious. When he heard about someone who had four or five children, he would growl, "an animal." Yet, I had a marvelous message from my father about sex. I was eleven years old and didn't know anything about sex, although I knew "you shouldn't touch it." I would get in the bathtub, take a bar of soap between my hands, and put my arms at a 45-degree angle touching the water. As I raised my hands, a film would fill in between my arms, and when my hands were about four inches out of the water, I moved my hands and arms in a semi-circular motion, bringing them back down to the water, forming a bubble about three inches in diameter. Then I would get an erection, and I would play submarine and torpedo the bubble, which I thought was great fun. There I was in the bathtub, the bubble had just broken, lying there with my little thing sticking out of the water, and my father walked in and said, "You shouldn't touch it, you'll get a disease." *But* his whole face lit up like a Christmas tree. He smiled, absolutely tickled, and I decided it was okay to play with myself. The nonverbal message he gave me was "Hey, that's great fun."

Curses

Early messages may take the form of curses. I had a client who had a learning disability (dyslexia) and didn't go to college. His father, a physician, used to tell him, "If you don't get a college education, you'll wind up shoveling shit." The client didn't go to college and became a successful kennel owner, cleaning up after dogs.

Hard to believe? Yes, I find it difficult myself. However, I had had over two thousand clients, and although these messages are not universal, they keep cropping up in people's lives.

I teach courses, and many teachers in the public schools give up their weekends to attend my graduate courses. One sixty-year-old teacher recalled that when she was small her parents always told her "get an education"; fifty years later she is still doing it (compliant).

Another teacher (rebellious) recalled that her father told her "Girls should not go to college." Forty years later she is still going to college to show him, even though he died many years ago.

I can recall that when I was little and had a bad day—I lost my bottle caps gambling, I fell and scraped my knees or tore my pants, the kids beat me up, or the teacher criticized me in school—I would come home sad and miserable. My mother would look at me and say, "These are the best years of your life." I would look at her, stunned, and think, "If these are the best years of my life, what's it going to be like later?" Of course when I got older, I suffered ten times worse and spent sleepless nights worrying.

How many readers have the curse "enjoy life now, because when you grow up and have rotten kids you'll know what it is to suffer." Being good little kids, we grow up, we enjoy a brief period of life when we're away from home, then we get married and have rotten kids and suffer, following our early message. How many were told, "You are just like your Uncle Willie, who was a drunk"; or like Aunt Thelma, who went crazy; or like Uncle Bud, the town buffoon.

Curses were known a long time ago, only the lingo was different. Our forefathers thought it was witchcraft. It wasn't witchcraft, just plain Mom-and-Dad-craft.

If, as a parent, I am such a wonderful magician, a witch, or a warlock, how come I could seldom get my kids to do what I wanted them to do? I only used my secret power, outside my awareness, to produce results I did not consciously want. It is necessary to be aware of the role that messages, advice, and early stories play in our programming, if we are to increase our options for happiness. This will be clarified in the next chapter.

Not all messages from parents are bad, of course. In this book, however, we focus on the bad. It's the same process when you go to the dentist. You don't talk about the thirty-five teeth that feel good. You talk about the thirty-sixth that hurts.

CHAPTER 5

Recognizing Messages:
Advice and Birth Stories

Advice

Most parental messages and advice and programming are designed for survival of the child. Most advice is good. The majority of parents want their children to be happy. Outside their awareness, however, they pass their programming to their children. Although the overt advice is intended for the child's happiness, the secret messages, given on a nonverbal level, work in the opposite way. Advice and secret messages have a figure-ground relationship. Hold the book about two feet away from you and look at Figure 1, until you can see a large three-letter word. This is an illustration of the figure-ground relationship. A major way we prevent ourselves from changing is by not seeing the total picture, by focusing either on the figure or on the ground.

For example, my mother advised me, "Always be honest," and when I grew up, I was. I prided myself on my honesty. My word was better than a gold bond, and I went through life thinking I was honest. After three years of psychoanalysis, it dawned on me that when Mom was saying, "Always be honest," the secret message might have been "Don't have

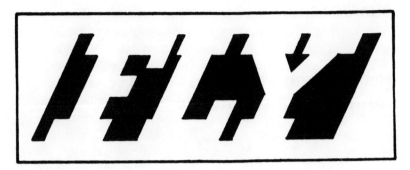

Figure 1
Ground Relation*

friends.'' I thought this because I had a grandaunt who was very honest and hypercritical. "Aufen Lunge ist aufen Zunge," which means whatever she thought she *said*. So anybody who walked in her house was immediately shot down: "Buddy, you're so fat." "Helen, you're getting old." "Lilly, that makeup makes you look like a prostitute." "Pauline, that hat looks like something the cat dragged in." I remember visiting my grandaunt with my grandmother, who had just had a heart attack. Grandmother asked for a little "schnapps" and my Tante Ethel said, "Humph, schika bist du?" ("So now you're an alcoholic?")

After another four or five years of three-times-a-week psychoanalysis, I changed my thinking about my honesty because I recalled (not relived) scenes. When I got caught lying, Mom would say, "Always be honest and tell the truth, and you won't get punished." I would lie because little kids lie naturally to avoid the dread punishment. So I would lie, Mom would repeat her honesty advice, and then I would get punished because I had lied. What if I told the truth? Usually I got punished anyway!!! So I decided that this message meant, "get yourself kicked, and don't defend yourself." From about age seven on, I developed a "guilty smile." If anything happened, in school or out, I would smile this smile and everybody would think I was guilty, whether I was or not. On one level the advice "Tell the truth," meant "Get your butt kicked." It wasn't until

*See footnote on page 34 for the answer.

after I left analysis that I finally found out what "always tell the truth" meant. It meant, "only tell me what I want to hear" and "don't tell me what I don't want to hear."

I remember my mother listening to a radio program, "The Illness of the Week" (I've forgotten the exact name of it). Each week a different illness was discussed: rheumatism, arthritis, phlebitis, colitis, bursitis, neuritis; after each program she would worry whether or not she had that illness. I couldn't have been more than six or seven when she came into the kitchen one day after listening to the radio. She looked at me very sadly and said, "Buddy, do you think I'm neurotic?" I didn't know what "neurotic" meant, but *I knew what to answer.* "Not you, Ma," I said. All you readers who pride themselves on your honesty—what was it you would never tell Mom or Dad when you were growing up?

Parents often give what appears to be conflicting advice. In decoding the family system, however, it becomes clear that the underlying secret message is almost always the same. The following are some clinical examples of parental advice.

"Be Careful"

Ted was a forty-four-year-old, good-looking guy. He lived in New York City, and his problem was that he couldn't make out with women. He had no problems getting dates, so I asked him what he did on the first date.

Ted: Well, I take her out for dinner, we talk, I find out about her background, where she went to school, what her parents do, what her interests are, and we talk.

Shep: What do you do on the second date?

Ted: Well, on the second date I usually take her to a museum. I like to see the paintings and find out what period the artist is from and that kind of thing. Sometimes we go to a concert or an art gallery and find out all about music and the composer.

Shep: What do you do on the third date?

Ted: They don't go out with me for a third time.

What he described was that when he goes out, there's no playfulness, fun, joy, or childlike interaction—going out with him is like going out with a computer. So I asked him:

Shep: What was your mother's favorite advice?
Ted: Well, her favorite advice was, listen to your father.
Shep: Anything else?
Ted: Yes, be careful.
Shep: What was your father's favorite advice?
Ted: Well, his favorite advice was, get the facts.
Shep: So you're still doing that. When you take a girl out, you're careful and get the facts. What do you want to do? Be careful and get the facts, or do you want to make out?
Ted: I want to make out.
Shep: Will you make a contract (set a goal) with me that the next time you date, you will not be careful and you will not get the facts?
Ted: Okay.

The advice from the mother was "be careful" and "listen to your father." Mother told him to be careful whenever he was going out, so the message was (1) the world is a scary place and (2) don't have fun, because if you're being careful you can't have fun. Furthermore, "Listen to your father" was the message "Women can't think!" The advice from the father, "Get the facts," duplicated the mother's message in that the "world is a scary place" and you'd "better get the facts."

Ted had good reason to believe the world was a scary place. Later in therapy he relived a scene where he was about seven months old and had had a loose bowel movement in his diaper. His mother had taken the dirty diaper and almost smothered him with it.

Incidentally, the client had a list of "don't feel" messages: "don't feel angry," "don't feel scared," "don't feel sad," "don't feel happy"; as a matter of fact, the only feeling he was allowed was that of depression. Being cut off from his feelings, he had to use his head, his computer, to process everything, so he was like Mr. Spock on Star Trek—emotionless.

Answer: The black sections of the figure on page 32 outlines the word FLY in white letters.

He was successful in his goal not to be careful and not get facts when he dated, but it took months before he felt comfortable having orgasms, i.e., letting go!

Advice to a Compliant Child

The mother's advice was, "Be good and people will like you." The father's advice was, "Don't bother people."

This person was trained to be compliant and went through life with low self-esteem. Since the mother was always telling him to be good, as a young child he must have thought, "Gee, I must not be good and I must be bad and the reason I'm bad is because I do all these things like laugh, play, and have fun." As a grown-up he was withdrawn, because if he was with anyone, he might bother that person, and he wanted to be liked. Nice guys wind up depressed, because instead of getting what they want out of life, they're busy being nice, doing the proper thing—always considerate of others but not of themselves. The programming was to feel depressed and resentful. If you are going through life being a nice guy (or girl), you can change and be a bad guy (or girl), and be happy.

Same Advice to a Rebellious Child

The mother's advice was "Be good and people will like you" and the father's was "Don't bother people." But the client was programmed to be rebellious and as a result he went through life being a pain in the "pratt!" He was invariably right and shot everybody down. He also felt unappreciated, since he was always trying to be helpful. People hated him. When he was with people, he constantly bothered them. He was very unhappy and felt angry/resentful because he wasn't liked. If you are going through life being miserable, you need to learn to be accepting and considerate (nice guy/sweetheart) and be happy. The exact same advice may have the opposite effect, depending on whether a child is programmed to be compliant or (defiant) rebellious.

"You Are Successful Only If You Are Married"

A young woman came in suicidal. She had nothing to live for; her sisters were all married, and she was involved with a

married man. She had no hope for the future or no hope of getting married. She felt she was a failure, alone and ugly.

This woman had a very successful career, and was attractive
and extremely capable. She identified an early child message as
"You are successful only if you get married." I asked her if her
parents had a happy marriage; she told me they were both
miserable.

She was still hearing what her mother had said and, following the message, was making herself miserable. She decided
to stop hassling herself and be successful without getting married.

When she took pressure off herself to get married, and stopped telling herself she was a failure, she became relaxed, and enjoyed being herself. She found she no longer needed her married
boyfriend to feel bad and swiftly dumped him. She made these
changes in less than ten weeks.

Recently I conducted a graduate course for a group of
teachers and lectured on advice for half an hour. The following
are some clinical cases from the discussion on parents' advice.

• "Mom said, 'Don't get upset, what do you expect?
They're only men.' She said this when I was upset over supposed injustices done to me by my three older brothers. She meant,
'You might as well not argue. It's a man's world, and a woman
has to know her place.' I felt angry and resentful and craved
membership in this magic male circle with its laughter and clever
discussions and deep voices. The men I have been attracted to
resembled one or another of my brothers. To this day I prefer-
red male companionship. That is, when we go out socially, I'll
sit with the men instead of the women. But I'll be angry and
resentful toward my husband."

• "Mom's main advice was 'Let me do it for you dear; let me
get you the . . .' She did this for everything throughout my
childhood and adolescence. Secret messages: (1) 'I am better
than you are.' (2) 'You are dependent on me.' (3) 'You're not
capable of doing anything'."

• "My father's advice was 'Try to do the best you can.' He
told me this in regard to school, jobs, and so on. The hidden

message must have been 'You can't be good enough and you're not as good as other people,' because I'm still trying hard to be the best, still trying hard to do the best I can, but never quite getting there.''

• "Mom's advice was 'Don't upset your father, he's tired. He works hard all day. *Don't bother him* with what we did all day.' This advice was given after an afternoon of shopping or after we had been visiting over coffee with the neighbors. As a kid, I used to wonder how it would upset him. The secret message must have been 'Don't tell, since I never tell anything.' My Dad's advice was 'Don't embarrass the family.' This was usually said when I was going on a date with a boy whose family my dad didn't know. I think his underlying message was 'Don't have a good time, because then you will leave and not be my little girl any more.' I left after college and have never lived closer than five hundred miles from my parents. But I am still cautious of close relationships with people, until I get the facts.''

Comment: Mom's advice is weird. "Don't upset your father," (after they had been having a good time) suggests "lie to him." The bottom line of Dad's advice seems to be "Watch out for yourself; the world is a scary place." His message seems to have been "Don't trust anybody and don't have friends." If that was the message, certainly the mother role-modeled it by being a liar. If she couldn't trust her own mother not to lie to her father, whom could she trust?

• "The advice was, 'Be good in school, work hard, get good marks, go to college, and become a somebody.' The secret message was 'The world is a scary place.' This message is still coming through to me. Here I am still furthering my education. I am a teacher; I take school seriously.''

Shep: On a hunch, the message was, "You're not okay, you have to make something of yourself." This constitutes a "Don't be you" message, if you spent your life making something of yourself.

• "My mother always said, 'The way you make your bed is the way you'll lie in it.' This was said when I didn't want to do something her way. The message was 'Do it my way or it will not turn out well for you.''

Shep: On a hunch, is this a message to foul up and suffer? Make your bed with cracker crumbs and then itch?
Teacher: And how.

• "Mom said, 'Be careful. Don't get hurt or you'll have to stay home.' This was a direct message: "The world is a scary place. Be fearful. If you stay home, you won't get hurt. Don't try anything new and don't do anything athletic! I don't do anything athletic."

• "My Mom always said, 'Be a fine, well-educated girl; make me proud.' The hidden message was 'Don't have fun; be serious; please me and feel guilty.' I'm living it. I'm mildly depressed all the time."

• My mother's advice was 'Be a good little girl and (do something for me).' The message was, 'You're not important in yourself, only in so far as you can please, conform, or serve.' I live this today, with low self-esteem, trying to please others for acceptance, and I have a need to be approved of."

• "The advice my mother frequently gave me was 'Don't waste time.' I have been productive all my life, and this course has created an awareness in me, and now I can take steps forward in changing my behavior."

• "My father's advice was 'Fight your own battles.' I think he meant 'Don't bother me with your problems, and don't complain; you're not important.' This has affected me all my life. I have a hard time asking for help. I fight with the administration; I fight with my wife; I fight with the school board. I'm constantly fighting."
Shep: On a hunch, this was more than advice, it was a curse. "Fight your own battles." How do you arrange to be always in combat?
Teacher: (After a minute of stunned silence) "My God, I do it to myself!"

• Teacher: Whenever I made friends with anyone, my parents would tell me, "Don't dog people's footsteps." I think the secret message was, "Don't have friends, and you're not important." Anytime we kids asked for help, they would say,

"God helps those who help themselves." If I got into an argument with anyone, they would say, "Turn the other cheek." When we had company, "Children should be seen and not heard." Every day I was told, "Do unto others as you would have them do unto you." When we were at my grandmother's house, "Be kind to your elders." Any time we were having fun, "Stop fooling around." And also, my mother used to say, "Wait till you're a mother." I think the bottom line was don't have fun; don't be yourself; please everybody in the world, and I don't know about that "wait till you're a mother'."

Shep: That's not advice, that's a curse. Usually it goes, "Wait til you're a mother and you'll know how I suffered." The message is to program your children so you can suffer and feel guilty and play martyr.

• "Mom used to tell me, 'Be friends with everyone, regardless of color or religion.' I believe the secret message was, 'Don't have friends,' because how can you be friendly with everybody?"

Shep: Have you been friends with everybody?

Teacher: No, I've had a whole series of friendships that always break up when they take advantage of me.

Shep: Will you possibly consider that the message is, "Don't stand up for yourself; you're not important. You have to be friends with everybody; their needs are more important than yours."

Teacher: That fits.

• "My mother said, 'Get your head out of the clouds' when I told her I wanted to be a poet. The hidden message was, 'Work like hell and don't enjoy it,' and I have done this."

Some clients do not remember their parents' advice. I ask them what advice they are giving their children. This is a great tool for parents to get in touch with the secret messages they are giving. It can also be a clue to the messages they were given.

What provoked parents to give the advice they did? It is usually the opposite part of the secret message and stands in a figure-ground relationship. Each case is different and depends on the individual and the specific situation. There is no cookbook of advice with secret messages.

Birth Story

Little kids often learn and make decisions about themselves by hearing grown-ups talk about them.

What did your mother tell your Aunt Ethel about your birth? And what did she tell you? Suppose Mom was in the habit of saying, "You were a breach baby. How you made me suffer!" The message may well have been, "You should feel guilty and make it up to me all your life for having made me suffer." Many of my clients respond, "But, I *was* a breach birth, and my mother *did* suffer. That's fact, not a secret message." When asked, however, most of my clients admit that they have had tremendous guilt feelings ever since they were kids.

Even if the story of suffering is true, it is not the child's fault; she neither chose the breach position nor enjoyed Mom's pain. Furthermore, many children are the result of difficult births, but not all mothers go through life talking about it, unless they are programmed to program their children with guilt.

Aside from feeling guilty, the message may be, "You shouldn't be here; look how you hurt me. You're only here on my tolerance." It's not unusual for people subjected to such comments to be depressed and to have had the thought when they were young, "I wish I was dead," or "They'll be sorry when I'm dead." They might also have fantasized, "These aren't my real parents, because if they were my real parents, they would like me." This constitutes a "don't be" message.

When a mother says, "You came thirty-six hours late and ruined my Fourth of July party," the messages may be, "You shouldn't be here; you're inconsiderate; look how you made me suffer; you're not important."

If the child is told, "I found you in the garbage," the message is, "You're garbage."

"You came at the wrong time, you should have been a boy," is a message of "You're not okay." Also, because the child was a girl, the message is, "Don't be you" and "Don't be a girl."

We haven't dicussed Dad in this system. If Dad is giving the little girl a lot of recognition for being a tomboy, for being tough, for doing boyish things, and if Mom is buying her a baseball mit and a bat instead of dolls, the little girl could have a serious problem later in life as a woman. The problem may be in decision making, because when she was very little, she could not decide whether to be a boy or a girl. There is a period early in the child's development when she thinks it is her choice whether to be a boy or a girl.

This is not to say all problems in decision making stem from early identity confusion. Often people who have trouble making decisions had some tough decisions to make when they were young, like "which parent to side with" if the child was in a tug of war between the parents, or the early game of corner, where the kid is cornered and no matter what he or she decides, he or she is ridiculed for the decision.

Kids pick up other messages also from a "difficult" birth. Frank was told that he was the result of a twenty-five-hour labor, but he finally made it. Frank went on, "I'm still very slow now, but I'm a real 'plugger.'* Things don't come easily to me, but I always finally get there." He has spent a lifetime following the pattern of his birth story. He had never before been aware of this connection, or the possibility that he could change it or do some things quickly, painlessly, without having to plug away at them.

Joanna's birth was also a long (twenty-four hours) and painful delivery for Mom. She heard the message; to "make it up" to Mother for having been guilty of giving her so much pain. "I learned to be good," she states. "Also, I recall I was a difficult child; nothing was ever easy." I asked her, "How do you arrange it so that 'nothing is ever easy'?" She got in touch with her perfectionisms and started making changes.

All sorts of birth stories impart secret messages to kids. "You were premature and when I brought you home you weighed only four pounds, so tiny and fragile-looking that I hardly dared touch you." The secret message here was, "You have the power to scare me." The client who told this to her daughter says that the girl lives up to her greatest expectations and scares the daylights out of her. She undertakes all sorts of dangerous activities, where she seem small and the risks are large.

*He did not intend a pun, and was unaware of the double meaning.

In another case, the birth had been a "posterior" one, usually causing a longer and more difficult delivery. The baby was born black and blue. Dad wrote in the baby book, "Let's start saving now for a plastic surgeon," a not so subtle message, "You are ugly!" The child is now fifteen years old and is in therapy. One of her problems is that she thinks herself ugly. The reality was that she is a stunning-looking girl, almost a classic Greek beauty, and extremely shapely. Mary, one of our staff members, has been working with her on raising her self-esteem.

When she would go to a party with her peer group, she would not keep eye contact with any of the boys and floated around looking creepy. Mary got her to change her hair style and maintain eye contact with boys, and several suddenly became interested in her. She also had a body posture by which she would stand with her shoulders slouched down and forward, so that she appeared far less bosomy than she actually was. In addition to changing her hairdo, she changed her body posture.

Which came first, this young person's raised self-esteem and the change in body posture and hairdo or visa versa? It's not important. Certainly getting the attention of boys helped raise her self-esteem, and as her self-esteem raised she dressed more attractively and her face glowed, instead of looking "sad and scared." Success breeds success, and small successes lead to great changes.

The most obviously painful and destructive messages and birth myths are usually related by psychotherapists. My mother enjoyed telling me and our relatives about my birth. She said, "I thought it was cramps and I almost lost you down the toilet." The reader can no doubt interpret the secret message. For many years after I became an adult, I would say, "When I die, just grind me up, flush me down the toilet, and send me out to the Harlem River. I don't believe in ostentatious funerals." It never dawned on me until recently that this was a reflection of my own programming, fitting right in with my birth story.

Bob, a psychiatrist, had an older brother, Charlie, who died at the age of eight, when Bob was two years old. While Bob was growing up, he often heard how Charlie was the good baby, if only Charlie would have lived, Charlie this and Charlie that. To

Mom, Charlie epitomized the essence of good. Naturally, Bob got the message that he just didn't measure up and that in order to be successful in Mom's eyes and have Mom really love him and appreciate him, the thing for him to do was to die.

Instead of dying, however, Bob stopped himself from living by going through medical school, internship, becoming a board certified endocrinologist, and then becoming a board certified psychiatrist—in an endless attempt to get approval for doing. Bob attended a few of our workshops, and as soon as he realized that he had been programmed to stop himself from living by being a slave and working, he stopped coming. When last heard from, he was out having fun and enjoying himself.

Another therapist, Alice, a PhD and a clinical psychologist, whose mother died giving birth to her, was told, "The doctor chose to save the baby and sacrifice the mother." Then Dad gave Alice to Grandma (Mom's mother) to raise. Grandma used to drag little Alice by the hand until she could stop a friend, a neighbor, a casual acquaintance, or even a stranger and relate her woeful tale—the tale of a wonderful daughter who always took care of her and bought her gifts and would have taken care of her for the rest of her life. Instead, the daughter had been killed giving birth to "this child," with whom poor Grandma was now saddled. At this point, Granny was usually weeping and the other adult was consoling her while a miserable, guilty little Alice stood by, waiting to be tugged along to the next such encounter: "When I went out with my grandmother, she would stop to speak to friends and refer to me as an orphan. It made me feel that I had an incurable birth defect and was not okay."

When Alice was about eight or nine, her father remarried, and took her to live with him, and her stepmother, who had children of her own; Dad didn't have too much affection for Alice. (He resented her for having "caused" the death of his first wife.) So Alice remained an outsider, a street waif among her own relatives. She knows that hers is a sad story and, like Grandma, she cries whenever she relates it. She is often depressed, but she never feels angry. She reported that the only time she felt good was when she was helping people.

She came in to supervisory training to learn how to be a better helper, and used to sit and take notes. You must understand that this is not the way people learn how to be effective therapists—by taking notes. Part of the requirements in training is that the therapist attend groups. Alice attended the first beginners' group and sat in the beginners' group taking notes, not relating to people, not giving or getting strokes, but remaining isolated. She lasted about three weeks and then left. I think she was firmly convinced that we were all crack-pots. In retrospect, I have to admit the possibility that I had something to do with her leaving; she was very, very much like my mother; I could have been more accepting and loving.

In examining birth stories, it is useful to tie them in with the other patterning, the feeling patterning, the thinking patterning, and the generational patterning, described in the following chapters. For example, one client said her mother used to tell her aunt that "her father didn't want her." She was forty-five years old, married, and had gone through life thinking that her father didn't want her.

She said that she had recently spoken to her father and learned that he had wanted her, that he'd never said that he didn't want her. She had grown up thinking that her father didn't want her, had married a man who didn't want her, and had had a miserable life.

I asked her what she thought Mom's secret message was; she replied that she realized now that her mother wanted her to be dependent and do what Mom wanted. She said, "My mother was angry and always yelling at my father. My father would hold it in and be resentful."

She was programmed to find men who resembled her mother, angry, hostile men, and then she would withdraw and restrain her resentment. By tying her birth story and the secret message into her life pattern, she was able to change.

Over and over again, I have observed daughters who have decided not to be like their mothers, sons deciding not to be like their fathers, but the message is always the same. In this case, it is "Don't be close" and "Don't have a warm, loving relationship." This was role-modeled by both parents, a message many of us have. We often manage to not be close, warm, loving, exactly opposite from the way our parent of the same sex did it, and thereby fail to see what we're doing. We need to be able to recognize the messages, in order not to blindly follow them like puppets.

CHAPTER 6

Early Childhood Nursery Rhymes, Songs, Fairy Tales, and Stories

Early stories, fairy tales, nursery rhymes, songs, and poems are indicators of programming. My mother used to love to read to me the poem about the Highwayman and Beth, the dark-eyed innkeeper's daughter, who waits at the inn for her lover. He subsequently is killed riding up to the inn. My mother's love for this poem stemmed from her programming; her father was a saloon keeper and she was dark haired and dark eyed. She always felt inferior to her younger sister, the blue-eyed, fair-haired beauty, and she was probably sad because her father, whom she idolized, adored her younger sister. She was programmed to feel sad and she therefore played martyr.

One of the biggest disappointments in her life (in living with this view of the world and her place in it), I believe, occurred when my father returned from World War I in 1919, alive and well. Somewhere, outside her awareness, she was probably "supposed" (programmed) to spend her life being a romantic figure (sad), grieving over her dead lover. Instead, she spent her life (sad), grieving over the fact that she married him and he wasn't successful.

One of the earliest songs I remember my mother taught me to sing went, "Just break the news to Mother/And tell her that I love her/And tell her not to wait for me,'' the dying soldier said. ''There'll never be another/To take the place of Mother/And tell her not to wait for me/For I'm not coming home!'' Dad had come home and she needed someone else to fill in so Mom could feel sad and play the martyr role. The secret message I received was, ''Go get yourself killed and I'll happily grieve for you forever.''

When I was four years old, I remember her playing on the piano another of her favorite songs, while I marched around the living room, ''Soldier Boy, Soldier Boy, where are you going?/To battle, to battle, to conquer the foe.'' Another of her favorites was ''The minstrel boy to the wars has gone, in the ranks of death you will find him,'' another young soldier who also went off never to return. Of course, neither she nor I was aware of the message. I was fortunate that my poor eyesight kept me out of aerial gunnery school in World War II or I might have lived up to Mom's expectations.

Nuts come in pairs, and Dad fit right in. When I was growing up during the depression, my father, unemployed, would sit around feeling depressed and suicidal. If he heard of somebody having a problem—for instance, if somebody had two flat tires—he would sigh deeply and say, ''He's better off dead.'' Only in later years did I see the ridiculousness of the statement, ''He is better off dead.'' As a child I heard this as a profound statement about life in general!

This was my father's projection, since he spent most of his life being suicidal. What kept him alive was his guilt: What would become of his poor children? I understand my father's feelings very, very well, since I spent many years in the same slot.

Figuring out the messages inherent in early favorite stories is interesting in more than one way. It is important to notice not only what stories and songs we remember, but what details we remember from the story. Two people may share the same story and remember different episodes, identifying with different characters and even remembering the plot very differently.

I remember that *Little Black Sambo* was one of my favorite stories. In it Sambo has beautiful clothes. He gives these to the tigers who threaten him and they chase each other around until they turn into pools of butter. Little Black Sambo scoops them up and takes them home to his mom, who makes pancakes to spread the butter on. He eats a large number of pancakes. For me, in this story, Little Black Sambo gives up his natural beauty in order to survive, and then Mom feeds him. I have had a weight problem most of my life. In order to survive when I was little, I had to give up my natural adornment, my natural beauty. Mom loved me very much, and was happy when she saw me eating huge quantities of food; it was her way of showing love.

Fred, a client, had a different reaction to the same fairy tale. He used to have nightmares in which he saw the enormous faces of two tigers and he would wake up terrified and in a cold sweat. Following an exercise consisting of writing about early stories, songs, etc. Fred realized that the nightmare resulted from "Little Black Sambo," a story which had thoroughly frightened him as a child because the tigers had chased him and threatened to devour him. After he associated the nightmare with the story, he no longer had nightmares. He realized that when he was little, Mom and Dad had been the tigers, two large, angry grown-ups, but now they have no power to devour him.

The most important factor here is not what the actual story said, but how it is remembered and the associations to what is remembered. Following are several clinical cases illustrating associations between childhood stories and later life patterns. Each client's reading and interpretation of a basic, well-known story is unique to his or her own situation.

• *Goldilocks* (1)

Shep: What's your favorite story?

Joe: *Goldilocks and the Three Bears.*

Shep: Tell me the story.

Joe: Goldilocks goes into a house and tries out different beds; one is too long and one is too short. Just then the bears come home, so she jumps out the window and runs away into the woods.

Shep: In what way are you going from bed to bed in your current life?

Joe: I go down to the Village and flirt with homosexuals, so I guess I go from bed to bed.

Shep: Is that the woods you're walking in?

Joe: Yeah.

Shep: There's a big danger to Goldilocks when the bears come home. What's the danger to you?

Joe: Well, I come on to some of these guys and then leave in a huff and one of these days I'm going to get myself killed.

Shep: Will you make a contract to stop walking in the woods and going from bed to bed? Get your excitement in safer ways?

Joe: Yes (big sigh). It will be a relief.

• *Goldilocks* (2)

Shep: What's your favorite story?

Pete: *Goldilocks*

Shep: Tell me the story.

Pete: Well, Goldilocks goes for a walk in the woods and she finds a house and there are chairs and there is porridge. This porridge is too hot, that one's too cold, this one's just right. Then she tries out the beds and this one's too hard, that one's too soft, and she finds one that's just right, and then the bears come home so she jumps out the window and runs away into the woods.

Shep: How does this tie into your current life?

Pete: Well, I like to go for a walk in the woods. I own a couple of hundred acres upstate and I really enjoy walking in the woods.

Shep: Okay, simple enough. What about the beds?

Pete: Yeah, I've been married and I'm breaking up my marriage, then I plan to try out a couple of different beds (laughs).

Shep: There's an element of danger in this when the bears come home. How does that tie in?

Pete: I still ski at my age and I'm fifty-five. I pilot my own plane. I've done a lot of dangerous things. I've been sky-diving.

Shep: Is this a life pattern?

Pete: Yeah. When I was a teenager, we used to climb cliffs in Niagara Falls. That was scary and one of the kids got killed. When I was in my twenties, I was sky-diving and one of the kids got killed.

Shep: I hear the pattern is to do dangerous things with somebody else getting killed. Is this a pattern where you do dangerous things and you come out okay, but some others don't?

Pete: Now that you mention it, it could be. I don't understand how I have anything to do with that, though.

Shep: You might think about that sometime. But back to Goldilocks. When you were little, what was going on in the house that you wanted to run away from and get away from?

Pete: My mother was impossible. I had a cousin, the same age as me, who lived nearby, and he would tell his mother everything that went on in school and she would tell my mother and then when I would get home from school, my mother would get on my case. I was always in trouble.

Shep: So being home was uncomfortable. How does this tie into your marriage?

Pete: I've always stayed away from the house whenever I could. I worked until 10 or 11 every night and then on weekends I worked around the house, but outdoors. Also, I'm on the board of my local church and have a lot of church involvement.

Shep: What I'm hearing now is a long-term pattern of not being in the house. What do you want for a contract? Or do you plan to spend the rest of your life staying away from whatever house is "the house" at the moment?

Pete: No! Definitely not. I want to feel comfortable without running away or feeling that anyone who is there with me is a bear. *Ha.* My wife is an angry bear. My divorce is definitely going through, but I'm tired of this pattern! I'm going to change.

• *Goldilocks* (3)

Jean: *Goldilocks* was my favorite.

Shep: What's the story of Goldilocks?

Jean: Well, it was suspenseful. You never know when the bears were going to come back. I never finished the story because I was too scared to find out how it ended. I still don't know how it turned out.

Shep: Is this a life pattern for you, where you scare yourself and then don't finish things?

Jean: Yes.

Shep: What small task can you think of that you can be scared of, yet finish safely?

● *Goldilocks* (4)

Morey: My favorite was *Goldilocks*. I identified with the baby bear.

Shep: The baby bear?

Morey: Yeah, he frightened Goldilocks out of her bed. When my mother was eight months pregnant, I hid in the closet and went "Boo!"

Shep: What happened?

Morey: She said, "Oh, Morey." But she never did anything like punish me. She did walk out of the room in anger, though. If she told me not to eat something, I ate it all, like porridge. It was more of a joke than anything. I guess I've never really grown up.

Shep: Does this cause problems for you?

Morey: It sure does. I'm still playing "tricks," kid stuff on people, especially women, and they are still leaving. I do it to get attention, but they run away. I think I'd like to grow up and try something new instead.

Let us look at a few of the variations on a different popular fairy tale, "Cinderella," to illustrate this personalizing tendency in another context.

● *Cinderella* (1)

Mary-Jane: My favorite fairy tale is *Cinderella*.

Shep: And what do you remember about it?

Mary-Jane: Her beautiful clothes when she went to the ball.

Shep: And I can see that you enjoy beautiful clothes yourself. (Mary-Jane is well dressed.)

Mary-Jane: Oh, yes. I love shopping, trying on, buying, and wearing lovely things.

Shep: Is this a problem for you?

Mary-Jane: Well, I don't want to change into wearing rags. There's one thing, though. I do spend too much money on clothes and have more clothes than I can really use. I sometimes have trouble paying my other bills.

Shep: Could you enjoy shopping and trying on many things but buying fewer?

Mary-Jane: I don't know. Yes, sure I could. I can try things on and parade around in them in front of the store mirrors. I could limit myself to buying one thing at a time.

● *Cinderella* (2)

Lonnie: *Cinderella* was my favorite.

Shep: Tell me the story.

Lonnie: Cinderella had a wicked stepmother and her fairy godmother turns her into a princess.

Shep: Whom do you identify with?

Lonnie: Cinderella.

Shep: Who was the wicked stepmother when you were little?

Lonnie: Well, my mother, I guess. I'm angry because she made me work so hard. I was the oldest of the family and I had to do a lot of caretaking while my sisters got away with murder.

Shep: Are you still caretaking?

Lonnie: Yes.

Shep: How can you start taking care of yourself? You don't need to give anyone the power of a wicked stepmother over you now.

Lonnie: (Laughing) That's right.

● *Cinderella* (3)

Marianna: *Cinderella* was the one I liked best.

Shep: What's the story?

Marianna: The main thing was that she wasn't allowed any

time. She could go out, but she had to be home early.

Shep: Is this a life pattern for you?

Marianna: Yes. I never give myself enough time to do any
thing.

Shep: How do you feel about this?

Marianna: Frustrated. And sad, too, because I always *have to*
go on to something else or go home just when I'm
starting to have fun.

Shep: Who is telling you that you "have to" leave when
you're having fun?

Marianna: Why, I just do. I always have other things I have to
do.

Shep: Who sets up the other things you have to do?

Marianna: I do. Of course, no one's making me leave; I set it up
so I have to leave. Wow! I could give myself enough
time for fun!

Shep: Yes, you *could*. How *will* you do that?

• *Cinderella* (4)

Cathy: *Cinderella* was my favorite.

Shep: Whom did you identify with?

Cathy: Well, I was an only child, but I didn't think I was
very pretty and I always liked to dance a lot, and
when Cinderella put on the gown and turned into a
beautiful thing and was dancing with the prince, it
was my fantasy.

Shep: Do you still think you're not a pretty girl, or act that
way? (The client, aged thirty-five, is a beautiful
woman.)

Cathy: Well, I know I'm pretty, but I don't feel pretty.

Shep: I'm surprised your story wasn't the *Ugly Duckling*.

Cathy: Oh, that was one of my favorites also.

"Sleeping Beauty" is another favorite with many people
that illustrates a pattern of "waiting" or wishful thinking.

• *Sleeping Beauty* (1)

Terry: *Sleeping Beauty* and *The Ugly Duckling* were both
favorites of mine when I was little.

Shep: And what is important about them for you?

Terry: Well, in both of them, the main character's beauty
          was either awakened or recognized at the end.

Shep: The main character slept, or suffered and felt sad, un-
          til suddenly, lo and behold, other, because of forces
          outside the heroine's power, recognized the beauty
          and caused a happy ending.

Terry: Right. I know what you are going to ask next. How
          long do I want to sleep or suffer and feel ugly before I
          wake up, take charge of my own beautiful life?

Shep: Yup. And what's the answer?

• *Sleeping Beauty* (2)

Fran: *Sleeping Beauty* was my favorite.

Shep: What's the story?

Fran: A wicked witch puts a curse on her and she pricks her
          finger and she goes to sleep for one hundred years and
          then Prince Charming comes and kisses her and she
          wakes up.

Shep: Are you waiting for Prince Charming?

Fran: Yes, I'm still waiting for Prince Charming.

Shep: And when Prince Charming comes, what kind of a
          guy goes around kissing women one hundred years
          old?

Fran: You're right. I'd better wake up and start enjoying
          real guys, instead of dreaming of fairy-tale princes.

In childhood favorites, you need to watch for what is important. In *Sleeping Beauty*, the Prince shows up to magically
awaken all the heroine's senses and love feelings. In real life, she
gets wrinkles with each passing year and she cannot begin to live
as a teenager after one hundred years.

In a Charles Dickens novel, there are 396 pages of pure
misery and in the last two pages everything turns out well. Not
so in real life. If we submit to 396 pages of pure misery, the
undertaker shows up on page 395 before any magical ending. So
we need to watch for and discover the important elements
within the story, and get the client to take charge of his or her
own ending, without spending a lifetime waiting for rescue.

• *Snow White* (1)

Shep: What's your favorite story?

Helena: *Snow White and the Seven Dwarfs.*

Shep: Did you get Prince Charming?

Helena: Hell, no!

Shep: What dwarf did you marry?

Helena: I married Dopey (laughs). I wanted to be Snow White because she was so beautiful, and I loved Dopey because he was so cute and lovable.

Shep: Do you still think he's cute and lovable?

Helena: No, I'm really mad at Dopey.

Shep: Snow White had a lot of responsibility. She was taking care of a lot of people. Do you do that?

Helena: Yes. And I'm tired of it.

Shep: And your husband can play Dopey to get you to take care of him?

Helena: Yes, I'm especially tired of that.

Shep: How can you stop taking care of him, so he will have to take care of himself?

Helena: Well, I could refuse to find his shirts and socks for him when he play helpless in the morning, and refuse to look up phone numbers for him when he acts confused and can't find them.

Shep: Great, will you do those things this week?

Helena: Yes. If only I can stop letting him be so helpless and dopey, he'd look a lot more like Prince Charming to me.

• *Snow White* (2)

Melanie: *Snow White* was my favorite story.

Shep: What's the story?

Melanie: She had to take care of a bunch of midgets.

Shep: What's going on in your current life that you're taking care of midgets?

Melanie: I teach first grade.

Shep: So every year you have a roomful of Bashfuls and Sneezeys and Dopeys to take care of?

Melanie: You know it! And nobody rides up on a white horse to take me off to a castle and a life of leisure.

Shep: Maybe no one ever will.
Melanie: I guess (sigh). I need a vacation. I guess if no rich
           prince will take me away, I'll have to arrange it
           myself.
Shep: Great. How can you do that?
Melanie: I have a friend who asked me to go along with her to
           the Caribbean during Christmas vacation. Maybe I'll
           go for a week around New Year's.

A few more case studies also applying to popular fairy tales
and children's books should give you enough experience in how
this exercise is done so that you can do this yourselves at home,
with your own favorites.

• *The Little Engine That Could*
Jeremiah: I loved the children's story about the train that
           thought it could and worked hard and made it up a
           mountain.
Shep: Who used to read that to you?
Jeremiah: My mother.
Shep: How does that tie into your father's advice?
Jeremiah: My father used to give me advice, "Try hard and put
           a lot of effort into it."
Shep: Do you still follow Dad's advice?
Jeremiah: Oh, sure. I feel like I'm always exhausted, always in
           the middle of an uphill struggle.
Shep: What could you do this week that would be easy,
           simple, a gentle slide downhill, instead of a struggle
           upward?
Jeremiah: All I can think of is to change the oil in my car.
           That's easy. It hardly seems hard enough.
Shep: Whoops! You're already trying to think of
           something harder, that would be a struggle.
Jeremiah: Okay, right. I'll change the oil and keep it simple.

• *Robin Hood*
Ed: *Robin Hood* was my favorite.
Shep: What's the story of Robin Hood?
Ed: He stole from the rich and gave to the poor.
Shep: How are you doing that?

Ed: I'm an accountant. I steal from the government and give to my poor clients.

Shep: How else?

Ed: I'm on several committees for social justice.

• *Hardy Boys*

Ed: My favorite story was *The Hardy Boys.*

Shep: Tell me about them.

Ed: Well, they were always solving problems.

Shep: Is this a life pattern for you?

Ed: Yeah, I'm always solving problems.

Shep: What do you do to make problems for yourself?

Ed: (Laughs) I make problems where they don't exist.

Shep: What do you want to do about it?

• *Heidi* (1)

Marla: My favorite story was *Heidi.*

Shep: Tell me about her.

Marla: She lived with her mean old grandfather and she helped a little crippled boy.

Shep: Who was the mean old grandpa when you were little?

Marla: My actual grandfather. My parents split up and I lived with my grandfather. He resented me.

Shep: Who's the crippled boy in your current life?

Marla: My husband. I'm helping him and resenting it.

Shep: Is this a pattern?

Marla: Yeah. I've spent most of my life, I'm a nurse, helping other people.

• *Heidi* (2)

Shep: Tell me your favorite story.

Nora: *Heidi.*

Shep: What's the story of "Heidi"?

Nora: Love conquers all things. The grandfather was an old and grumpy rescuer, and after Heidi went to live with him she did a total transformation and turned him into a loving person. Then she had this little crippled boy, his name was Peter, and she taught him how to read. She just spread love all over the world.

Shep: Will you share with the group your occupation?

Nora: I teach emotionally disturbed children.
Shep: So you're spreading love all over the world?
Nora: Yeah.
Shep: Are you getting your needs met?
Nora: No. I meet everybody else's needs, but I don't get my own met.

• *Bambi* (1)
Shep: What's your favorite story?
Doris: *Bambi*
Shep: What's the story of Bambi?
Doris: I'll make it short. He was born in the forest and his father got shot by a hunter and his mother died in a forest fire, but Bambi grew up and made it.
Shep: Who did you identify with, Bambi?
Doris: Of course.
Shep: What happened in your life where you lost somebody?
Doris: Nothing.
Shep: Be Bambi.* How old is Bambi?
Doris: Four.
Shep: What was going on in your life when you were four?
Doris: Oh, my Dad went into the army and my mother had to go to work to support us four kids.
Shep: (On a hunch) Bambi was an orphan. Did you feel like an orphan or abandoned?
Doris: Yes. I feel my husband has abandoned me.
Shep: Interesting. I asked did you feel abandoned, not do you feel abandoned. Is this a life pattern?
Doris: Yes.
Shep: What can you do so as not to feel abandoned?

• *Bambi* (2)
Ted: My favorite story was "Bambi." I saw the movie when I was eight years old, and it's my favorite movie to this day. I adore it.
Shep: What is the main thing about Bambi?
Ted: Well, he suffered and then he grew up and made it.

*A Gestalt technique, the person pretends to be Bambi.

Shep: Are you still suffering?
Ted: Yeah.

• *Jack and the Beanstalk* (1)
Tom: My favorite story is *Jack and the Beanstalk.*
Shep: What's the story?
Tom: A guy goes out to get a cow to sell so they can get money to buy food. He comes back with beans and his mother is very angry and throws them out the window. Overnight, bingo! the beanstalk. He climbs it and . . .
Shep: Hold it. So Jack is in the business of getting Mom angry. Who are you getting angry in your current life?
Tom: My wife.

• *Jack and the Beanstalk* (2)
David: *Jack and the Beanstalk* was my favorite.
Shep: What's the story?
David: I felt that Jack had a very heavy responsibility because he had to be the breadwinner.
Shep: How about you?
David: Yup, I have a heavy responsibility, or I make things my responsibility and never have any fun.

• *The Little Dutch Boy*
Art: *The Little Dutch Boy* who saved the town by keeping his finger in the dike was my favorite.
Shep: What finger are you keeping in the dike in your current life?
Art: Well, I've been wanting to leave my wife, she's crazy, but I'm afraid if I do she'll go all to pieces.
Shep: In the story, the little boy gets massive praise for heroism. Who is going to applaud your self-sacrifice?
Art: Nobody, I guess, though people do praise me for putting up with her.

The client was not aware of his contribution to keeping his wife crazy. This was one of the few marriages I worked to break up. He finally left his wife, and she went into therapy and made enormous changes in herself. His okayness was dependent on his staying in the rescuer slot and playing martyr.

Oddly enough, after he left her, he experienced fear of abandonment and begged her to take him back. She'd had enough years of playing crazy so he could rescue her, and threw him out. He then came into therapy and for the first time really worked to change himself. Before this, he had come to therapy to learn how to be a better rescuer and how to live with his "crazy" wife.

• And a Nursery Rhyme

Suzie:	I thought of the nursery rhyme of *Jack and Jill.*
Shep:	What's the story?
Suzie:	Jack and Jill went up the hill.
Shep:	Which one did you identify with?
Suzie:	Jill.
Shep:	What's there about that?
Suzie:	I'm a follower, not independent. If somebody falls down, I fall down, that kind of thing.
Shep:	So, Jill was dependent on Jack?
Suzie:	Oh, yes, or on anybody.
Shep:	What's going on in your current life?
Suzie:	I'm very dependent on my boyfriend.
Shep:	It's not so terrific to follow someone all the time, especially falling down. Besides, you always have to do what they want then, not what you want.
Suzie:	That's true. I want to stand on my own two feet from now on.

All cases illustrate projection. We always project our own internal meanings onto outside events and stories. Evidently Sigmund Freud was turned on by the story of Oedipus from the classical Greek play *Opedipus Rex.* Oedipus, you recall, kills his father and marries his mother, and for Freud, this must have fit very strongly. So he proceeded to project this story onto the entire world as a universal theme in all our minds.

In the Freudian psychoanalytical system, every single one of us men has a desire to kill our father and marry our mother.

Every woman has a corresponding Electra complex (the term also comes from the classical Greek play of the same name); she wants to kill her mother and marry her father. In the Freudian system, however, unless you get in touch with Oedipal feelings, you are "blocking" or showing "resistance" to getting better. But in my experience, I would say that out of two thousand clients, I have had perhaps four or five with an Oedipus/Electra complex. It is not universal.

I hope you have found these indicators of programming interesting, and will consider thoughtfully the next three chapters on programming, which discuss other ways of how we are programmed.

CHAPTER 7

Role Modeling—Generational Patterning

In our awareness, we usually do not have those characteristics we disliked in our parents. *Outside our awareness,* we very often are just like our parents.

My great-grandfather lived in poverty in czarist Russia. He was a very stern, bitter man. Devoutly religious, he was always either at home studying the Scriptures or at the local synagogue, praying (compulsive scholar/"workaholic"). He "looked through" people, unless they were Talmudic scholars. Very slow and deliberate, he spent his life waiting (compliant) for the coming of the Messiah. (See Figure 2 for a summary.) He was not close to his family; he spent his life depressed and withdrawn. Historically, Talmudic scholars don't make it. His wife was an angry woman; she had to earn the living for the family and raise eleven kids while he studied and prayed.

My grandfather decided he was not going to be anything like his father, so he moved to America in 1885 and became a reporter for a Jewish newspaper. He was antireligious, and intellectual, and a scholar. He was always in a hurry to get things done and impetuously bought a farm in Connecticut in the hope of relieving his asthma, only to discover that his work kept him in New York City. My grandfather neglected his family, lived it up in New York, played cards with his cronies, drank, and gambled; he was never at home. In those days, reporters didn't make it, and he spent a good part of his time worrying about losing the farm and being depressed because he was not at home. He went home once a year to knock up his wife. (He had three wives; in those days, men outlived women.) His wives were very angry women. They had to run the farm and raise the kids without help, and they lived in poverty.

My father decided he would not be anything like his father. My father was a stern, religious, plodding, bitter man. Behind his back, he was known as *Der Sauer*, "the sour one." He spent his life waiting for the undertaker; depressed, always at home and worried about work during the depression. He didn't make it; he went through three years of medical school, enlisted in the army in 1917, and never finished his education. My mother was a very angry woman; all my father did was sit around the house, depressed. My parents were very poor, whereas all my mother's brothers were rich.

I decided I would never be like my father. I was never at home, was not religious, was impetuous, was a workaholic, and was rebellious to authority figures; today I find myself a writer, like my grandfather. I didn't make it, by finishing college, receiving three degrees, and leaving the field for which I had prepared. I spent most of my life depressed and suicidal, worrying about making a living, not close to my family, withdrawn, and married to an angry wife—following the footsteps of my father, grandfather, and great-grandfather.

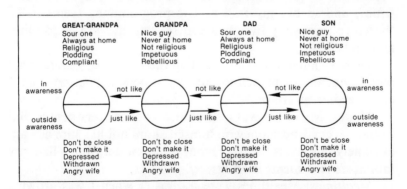

Figure 2
Selective Perception

Figure 2 is, of course, a simplification. Since the male line was programmed not to get angry at women, wives, or daughters, they could get angry at their sons. In analytic terms, they were programmed to be "passive" and pick "aggressive" spouses.

It is too early to tell about my son because he is not married yet. However, about three years ago he called from Chicago where he was in college, and spent about a half hour talking to my wife—this was very, very unlike him. Finally I got on the phone and said, "Jared, what's the matter?" He said, "I'm having troubles with my girlfriend." I said, "Don't tell me, let me guess, she is mad at you!" He said, "How did you know?" I said, "You're my son. What did you do to make her angry at you?" I worked with him to make him aware of what he was doing to make her angry.

I come from a long line of weak men, who team up with strong, angry, hostile women. If they are not angry or hostile when they meet me, they will get that way in no time at all.

There was a time-release message in the programming. After his second wife died, my grandfather, at the age of sixty, remarried and was relatively happy. My mother died when my father was sixty-five. It was amazing to see the metamorphosis that came over him. He was like a teenager: happy, dating, joyful. He remarried at the age of sixty-seven, and his widow still speaks of what a great lover he was. This, of a man who had spent his entire first marriage depressed and withdrawn. Moreover, my grandfather became financially secure in his late fifties, and so did my father. The programming seems to be "after you are sixty-five, you can start to live life, enjoy life, and make it."

There is much more to be said on the subject of generational patterning, and I will mention just a few personal patterns that I have become aware of.

Money: My father was a skinflint, pinched every penny, and would never spend money on himself. I am not like him as I am extremely generous, spend money like water, but, like my father, *do not spend it on myself.*

Mealtimes: Mealtimes were a disaster when I was growing up. My mother would cook something I didn't like, split pea soup, for example. She would serve me half a plateful and insist I try it. I would take a spoonful and gag. She would say, "Try a little more." Finally, my father would get angry and growl, "Eat your soup." I was terrified and would eat it with tears streaming down my cheeks. I swore I would never do that to my kids.

When my son was growing up, my wife would nag him at the dinner table, usually about school, and go on and on. Finally, I would get angry and growl at him. I realize now it was my wife I was angry at, but I couldn't admit it or express it to her. I wanted her to shut up, not him. In retrospect, these must have been the same dynamics for my father.

My mother was a cold, emotionless nag. Nag, nag, nag. I swore I would never be like her. My father never nagged. He would tell me to do something once, twice was maximum, then he would become an angry, homicidal maniac. I decided I would not be like him.

I was right, I am not like either of them. I find I have become an angry nag.

The importance of learning how we are programmed and how programs are transmitted is that once we are aware, we can proceed to change our programming. We were not born angry/depressed/scared/guilty/resentful/frustrated/homicidal/suicidal, nor did we catch it on a toilet seat in Grand Central Station. There is no point in blaming ourselves for how we have programmed our children, nor in blaming our parents for how they programmed us. Who is to blame? Grandmothers and grandfathers, great-grandfathers and great-grandmothers, great-great-grandfathers and great-great-grandmothers? The important thing is to change ourselves so that we are happy, joyous, creative, self-fulfilling people, so that we set examples (nonverbal) and give good time messages to our children.

We can spend years in one position and then move to another, so that we may have permission to be happy until we are forty and then live a miserable life, or vice versa.

For example, a female client spent an entire loveless married life eighty pounds overweight. At the age of fifty-two, she divorced her husband, lost seventy pounds, and cut loose. At the age of fifty-two, her father had left her mother and cut loose from a loveless marriage. Of course, in some of her programming she was like her mother, too. This is true of all of us.

Time messages are given *by example*, by parents' role modeling, and also by direct verbal communication. You can see a little child about seven years old going out to play. Mother asks, "Where are you going?" Child answers, "Out to play." Mother says, "Aha, first clean your room, do your homework, take out the garbage, and straighten your dresser drawers, then you can go out to play. It's four-thirty now; be sure to be home by six for supper." Later in life, when that child is forty, fifty, or sixty years old, he or she will have a long list of things to do every day, the last of which will be something he or she really wants to do: to play, to enjoy himself or herself, to be happy. The list will have twenty items, only fifteen of which may be accomplished. The programming is *after: after* you reach eighty, you can relax and enjoy life; *after* you have a heart attack, you may take it easy; *after* your children are grown, you may enjoy yourself; *after* your grandchildren are grown, you may enjoy yourself; *after* the great-grandchildren are seen safely through college, you may enjoy yourself.

In examining generational patterning, it becomes obvious why grandparents and grandchildren have such a good relationship: *they have a common enemy*.

Generational programming has proved to be a superb tool in couple and family counseling. I will illustrate from a clinical case, but first I want to mention that in retrospect, to my surprise, many clients reach awareness easily, as shown in the following examples. There are exceptions, especially when the client at a very early age was terrified or abused and battered by the parents.

Shep: Tell me about your husband.
Sue: My husband is a real SOB. He's constantly putting me down and criticizing me. He gets angry at the drop of a hat, and he won't do anything I want him to do, and he never takes me out. He spoils our daughter rotten, and he's always putting down and criticizing our son, who's a good boy.
Shep: How is he like your father?

Sue: He's nothing like my father. My father was warm, kind, loving, gentle. He never put me down, never criticized me. I was the apple of his eye, and he would do anything for me.

Shep: How was your father in relating to your mother when you were growing up?

Sue: Oh, to my mother he was a SOB. He constantly put her down, he criticized her and he'd get angry at her at the drop of a hat. He never did anything she wanted him to, and he never took her out.

Shep: So, in essence, you "married" your father?

Sue: Yes.

Shep: How did your mother get even with your father?

Sue: She didn't. She just put up with him for our sake.

Shep: How did she persecute him?

Sue: Well, I guess she was withdrawn, and they didn't have much of a sex life. Also, she was the world's worst cook, which is funny because Grandma was an excellent cook. Dad was a finicky eater, and so Mom would either burn the roast or overcook the vegetables, or put too much salt in the soup. Mealtime was usually a disaster. Mom was always sad and was a wet blanket on everything. She was always sick and having backaches and headaches.

Shep: How do you persecute your husband?

Sue: I guess I'm withdrawn, and we don't have much of a sex life. He always wants sex and I never want sex.

Shep: How often do you have sex?

Sue: Once a week, once every two weeks.

Shep: So you make it a no trip or a bum trip?

Sue: I guess so.

Shep: What about the cooking?

Sue: I'm an excellent cook.

Shep: Mealtimes are happy?

Sue: Not exactly. My husband has this thing about buying. He's not stingy or frugal in some areas, but when it comes to buying I always buy the name brands, and they cost a few pennies more. He goes absolutely bananas when he hears the food bills. Also, mealtime

	is the only time we really get to talk, and I usually tell him about what the children did or things that need taking care of, and he gets very angry.
Shep:	So, that's how you drive him bananas. Drive him up the wall, just like Mom use to drive Dad?
Sue:	Yes, I guess so.

When little Sue was growing up and she saw the relationship between her parents, and *in her awareness,* her father was kind, warm, and loving to her, she chose a man like her father. Outside her awareness, she decided that she would find a man just like her father, someone who would be angry, hostile, and critical of her, and put her down and then she could get to persecute him by withdrawing and not having sex. What Sue wanted the most, which was a warm loving relationship, is what she proceeded to stop herself from having. Let's interview Stanley, the husband, and see his side of it.

Shep:	How is Sue like your mother?
Stanley:	She's the exact opposite. My mother was an angry, hostile witch. She constantly put me down, criticized me.
Shep:	How was your father? What kind of person was he?
Stanley:	Oh, my father was warm, kind, loving, gentle. He never put me down or criticized me. I was the apple of his eye, and he would do anything for me.
Shep:	How was your mother's relationship to your father?
Stanley:	Well, my Mom was constantly putting him down, criticizing him. She'd get angry at him at the drop of a hat, and always said that he spoiled me rotten.
Shep:	So Mom was a big persectuor? Well, how did your Dad act toward Mom?
Stanley:	Well, he held two jobs. He worked so that he was hardly ever home, and when he did come home he was very tired. On weekends he'd be busy, or he'd take me out, and I guess their sex life wasn't so great.
Shep:	How are you like your mother in your relationship to Sue?
Stanley:	I'm just like her.

Shep: And how is Sue just like your father? In your father's relationship to your mother?

Stanley: Oh wow! She's depressed. My father was depressed. She withdraws. My father withdrew.

Shep: So you married your father, and now you're running Mom's pattern.

Stanley: Yep!

What Stanley wanted the most, a warm, loving relationship, is what he stopped himself from having by persecuting Sue.

It's not always true that we marry our mother if we're men, or that we marry our father if we're women.

A question I have been asked often is, why is it that before we were married, we had such a great relationship, and afterward it went sour? The answer is that before marriage or coupling, our role models are romantic models: Hollywood, novels, the movies, television. After we are couples or are married, the role model is our mother and father and outside of our awareness, we recreate our parents' relationship.

Many factors other than role modeling, are involved in our becoming the person we are. One of them is early life experience.

CHAPTER 8

Man, The Robot—
Early Life Experiences (Scenes)
That Act as Electrodes

Electrodes

The experimental psychologists discovered that they could implant little wire electrodes in parts of a monkey's brain, and when they threw a switch, sending a mild current through the animal, the little monkey would jump, scratch, get hungry, or exhibit various types of sexual behavior.

Very early life experiences that contain enormous emotional content, scare or pain, may function in us as electrodes. Wilder Penfield, a neurosurgeon, using a weak electric current, stimulated the temporal cortex of patients he was operating on, and found that all of us have a complete recording, like a videotape, of all our experiences from birth. Each recording contains the emotions we felt at that time, and is continuous and sequential. He reported:

> The subject feels again the emotions which the situation originally produced in him, and he is aware of the same inter-pretations, *true or false*, which he himself gave to the experience in the first place. Thus evoked, recollection is not the exact photographic or phonographic reproduction of past scenes or events. It is the reproduction of what the patient saw and heard and felt and understood (at that age).*

*W. Penfield, "Memory Mechanisms," AMA *Archives of Neurology and Psychology*, (1952), Volume 67.

Electrodes come in two forms: imprints and introjects.

Imprints

Imprints are early memories fixed in the mind, having great influence on us, and usually not in our awareness. The most striking examples of imprints are in the animal kingdom. Salmon, for instance, are imprinted with the location of their ancestral stream.

Konrad Lorentz, a biologist, discovered that when a baby duck hatches, it thinks that the first object it sees is its "Mommy." Lorentz would wait until the ducklings hatches, let it see him, and it would then follow him around and respond to him as though to its Mommy.

A biologist recently reported that he approached an antelope giving birth to twins in the wilds. The first twin born saw her mother, froze, and crouched low in the grass as the biologist approached. The mother dropped the second twin and fled; this twin opened her eyes, saw him, and proceeded to follow him. He reported he had a heck of a time getting away from the baby antelope.

Imprints are not logical in the sense of grown-up logic. The are preverbal, usually under the age of eighteen months. Occasionally an imprint can occur when the child is older if it has enormous energy input. For example, one client relived a scene of being beaten almost to death with a steel poker by his father at *age six*! Thereafter, when faced by authority figures, he would freeze.

Imprinting can be very mild, or not affect us in "living." My first day of kindergarten, I had a complete set of rules to follow. "Don't get dirty, behave yourself, raise your hand if you have to go to the bathroom, pay attention to the teacher, cross at the crossing where the guard is, come straight home, don't get into fights with other kids, and be good" (whatever good meant—do what I tell you, not what you want to do).

I looked forward to going to kindergarten with excitement. First, anything was better than staying in the house with my mother, who would let me go outside to play for an hour and then bring me upstairs and change my clothes for clean ones. Secondly, it meant that I, a younger child, was now grown up. I behaved myself, and I was also fortunate that I had a lovely teacher, Mrs. Fleming. I remember that day so clearly because of what happened.

My mother sent me to school wearing a one-piece, short-sleeved, short-pants, jump suit (and I didn't have any underwear on). The suit was yellow with big buttons. In the back of the suit was a flap with three big buttons. During class I had to "make," so I raised my hand and told the teacher that I had to go to the bathroom. (I had not yet learned that phrase, "May I leave the room?") She said yes and gave me a big, wooden pass, and I went to the john, which was down the hall. I couldn't reach the middle button on the jump suit. I couldn't get the damn middle button unbuttoned and I couldn't get the suit off! I tried to squirm out of it, but that didn't work either. My options were either to ask the teacher to unbutton me or make in my pants. I ran back in the classroom and went up to the teacher in front of the whole class and asked her to unbutton me. She did and then I ran back to the bathroom, and then holding the flap so that my rear end wouldn't show, I ran back to the class and she buttoned me up.

This was probably the most embarrassing experience I have ever had. The kids were very nice and didn't laugh at me. Since it was their first day of school, they probably were sitting there fully programmed for this momentous occasion.

I have a full color eidetic (vivid) memory trace of that yellow jumper with the big buttons. I can close my eyes and see it. The buttons looked about three inches across. Of course, they weren't. They probably were more like one-inch buttons, but to a small child, everything looks larger than it is. Strange, I never wear anything yellow today. I have no yellow shirts, sweaters, or pants, have never owned a yellow car, and I once got a yellow tie as a present and never wore it. Oddly, I like yellow. It is one of my favorite colors. I was not aware of this imprint until I was writing this book.

The indications are that we are far less autonomous than we believe. Our tastes, choices in color, music, art (lack of taste) may be programmed into us.

Unlike my jump-suit experience, not all imprints are mild. Some can have quite severe effects, as you will see in the following examples. But before giving these examples, I would like to comment on the clinical case experiences you will be reading about. If you have never had any experience reliving scenes, you will have difficulty in believing it possible.

The clinical examples are edited from tapes, some of which were very long pieces of work, up to two hours. Some scenes the client reached only after many false starts and detours. Early scenes usually are an end product of therapy after the person has made significant changes. Some examples are verbatim and are startling in their brevity. Unbelievable, but true, that a person could spend years stuggling with a problem, and after years of therapy, can reach solutions, can change, and can be "cured" (cured of that problem) in a ten-minute or twenty-minute piece of work.

Where necessary, I have made the dialogue concise for the sake of readability. In all cases the names have been changed, and in some cases the sex has been changed, so that "he" may have been a "she" and vice versa. This has been necessary to protect the identities of the clients.

Clinical Examples

• The client, aged thirty-three, is a fifth-degree black belt. Using regression analysis,* he reports: "I'm an infant. I'm in a perambulator. There is a netting over it." (Client screams.) "A wasp stung me!" After the client is rested and is out of regression:

Shep: How has this affected your life?
Client: I've been scared all my life. I've got an arsenal at
          home (client is a gun collector). I carry weapons of
          one kind or another. I spend twenty hours a week on
          karate.

After reliving the scene, the client changed his perception of the world as a place where everyone was out to get him.

• Another client, aged forty-eight, came into therapy because he was having urges to kill his children and then poke out his right eye with a scissor. He had a history of hurting himself on the right side—walking into sharp objects, always on

---

*S. Gellert, "Regression Analysis," *Transactional Analysis Journal* Vol. 4, No. 4, (1974). The term regression as used here means that the client is relaxed and is enabled to relive very early scenes, as opposed to "recall" or "remember." The full sensory and emotional content is reexperienced.

the right side; cutting himself severely while shaving, always on the right side. After four months of individual and group therapy, he was in touch with many early scenes he had blocked out of awareness, for example, mother toilet-training him at the age of nine months by pinching his nipples and genitals, as well as other abuses by both parents. Having this awareness, he now wished to kill his parents instead of himself, and *then* poke out his right eye. In another month of therapy he had forgiven his parents, but still had the urge to poke out his right eye.

The client was regressed and reported the following:

Client: I'm being held down from behind. I'm an infant. I see my grandmother's face. (Frightened voice) She is coming closer! I see her teeth. She is going to bite me! She is going to bite my right eye! (Voice of disgust) Eeuch! She stuck her tongue in my eye! (The client was then brought out of regression.)

Shep: (After the client is rested.) Was Grandma from Russia?

Client: Yes. How did you know?

Shep: In Russia, when an infant or child has something in his or her eye, the grandmother, or perhaps a nurse, uses her tongue to clean the eye out. I understand they still do it today. (The client makes no comment.)

The following week the client reported that he had spoken to his parents and discovered that his grandmother had cleaned his eye with her tongue. He reported that he no longer had the urge to blind himself. The imprinted pattern was to feel rage, then scare, and then to wish to blind himself.

• Another client, aged fifty-five, was extremely rigid and had made few changes in a year of therapy. Each time she was regressed she would become stiff, with her hands spread out and her legs spread apart. She finally relived an early scene and reported as follows: "I'm an infant. I'm in a sink, and I'm holding onto the sides."

She later spoke to her mother, who told her that when she was an infant she was bathed in the kitchen sink in cold well water, and she was always terrified. After this the client accepted a major promotion. She had been hanging on to her low-ly position for dear life.

• One client's goal was to "play." In regression his arms started to wave and he reported a tingling sensation in his hands. He related a scene when he was about eighteen months old in which he had received an electric shock from an exposed wire. After regression and the electrode was discharged, the client then reported that he was able to relax and play, although the decision "it's not safe to play" which he had reached in therapy months before, was made at the age of four.

My experience has been that if a client has been imprinted, all the therapy in the world is not likely to help unless he is regressed, the early scene is relived, and the electrode is discharged. The energy locked in these memory traces is enormous.

The most dramatic change I have seen in a client is recounted in the following:

Client: My husband and I were discussing separating. He got angry and I got so scared. I took the children and left, even though my lawyer told me I should stay. I'm scared he will kill me. (Husband had no history of violence and had made no threats, and it is unlikely he would even strike her.)

In regression she suddenly goes rigid, her body arches up, she places one hand on her hip and one on her head, screams, and then cries.

Shep: What is going on?
Client: My God, my grandmother threw me through a window! I was a baby.

At the next session the client reported she had spoken to her mother and gotten details as soon as she left the group. When the client was a year old, her grandmother had gotten very angry at her brother while holding the client. She had chased him and had tripped and fallen near the window in the living room. The client went through one of the panes, her hip hung on the frame, and she needed stitches in her scalp.

The client reported that the day after the session, she moved back with her husband and told him if he didn't like it, he could move out. She had been imprinted, and below the level of her awareness she had been scared that if he got angry, he would throw her out the window. The reality was that he was scared of her and would never abuse her. The client, who had been nonassertive, a mouse, is a successful real estate salesperson today.

Very few cases are this dramatic. Women who are imprinted to be scared of men or men who are imprinted to be scared of women are usually in the business of getting members of the opposite sex to become angry at them in an effort to resolve the early trauma. Once "cured," that is, once the electrode is discharged, they may have to learn a complete set of social skills, which can be scary in itself if you have never gone through the "normal" teens and are 30, 40, 50, or 60 years old and are a "psychological" virgin or wallflower.

Introjects

Introjects usually occur after the age of two, and it is as if a piece of videotape had been spliced into a reel. It doesn't belong there.

When the early scene is reexperienced, Mom's or Dad's voice repeating the exact words, spoken in the same voice, will come out of the mouth of the client, even though the client may be in a regression as a very young child.

If you have ever had an experience in which you blew your stack, yelled at your children, and heard Mom's or Dad's exact voice or tone coming out of your mouth, that was an introject. Usually we then feel remorse because we swore we would never treat our children that way.

The following examples illustrate introjects:

• The client, aged thirty-six, had a goal to "stop acting like a witch just before I have my period. I'm a real bitch; I can't stand anybody, not even myself."

In regression, I said, "Get the miserable feeling of disgust. When did you have that feeling when you were young? Maybe something to do with bleeding?" She relived the scene and reported:

Client: I'm seven years old, and my mother is chasing me around the dining room table. Mom hits her eyebrow on the edge of the buffet and she's bleeding. (An angry, harsh, grown up voice; Mom's voice): "I'll get you! You'll never get away from me! You're rotten, you no-good kid! I'll kill you!"

After this work the client reported that she was able to stop thinking that something terrible was going to happen every time she got her period, and was able to remain calm and cool the week before her period, *but when she started menstruating*, she became a witch and was angry at everyone.

Using regression analysis she relived a scene when she was two and one-half years old and stuck a lollypop stick up her vagina and bled. Her mother's voice came out of her mouth in regression: "You rotten kid, you no-good kid. I'll kill you if you ever do that again." This was accompanied by a beating. Little kids are always sticking things in the various openings: eyes, ears, nose, rectum, vagina, but few parents respond as homicidal maniacs.

The client had Mom's angry tape spliced into her memory banks and, when symbolically "bleeding," would run "angry Mom" either on herself or on others.

• Another client, aged thirty, would go into a blind panic and want to run out of wherever she was, for no particular reason. In regression she reported a scene that occurred when she was four years old. She said, "I am sitting on a balcony and my mother comes over to me. She is angry." (In a loud, grown-up voice; Mom's voice) "You lousy rotten kid, you'll be the death of me yet. Someday I'm going to kill myself, and it will be your fault, and when I do it, I'll come back and haunt you.' "

The client reported that at age four she had broken her doll and that several days later her mother had indeed committed suicide by leaping off the balcony. Subsequent to reliving this scene, her panic stopped.

A weird phenomenon is that on some occasions when the introject comes out, an evil presence is felt and group members report experiencing chills. Once in a great while someone will have a "witch laugh" and when the person gives a certain laugh, group members report chills or discomfort—shades of witch-craft. As Albert Einstein said, "As the circle of light (knowledge) gets larger, so does the ring of darkness."

Fortunately, electrodes (introjects and imprints) are not common. Once the client has *relived* the experience and has felt the early emotion (pain, terror, suffocation), and the energy is out, the electrode is discharged.

Until an electrode is discharged, we may function like robots and limit our options, even though we know better!

CHAPTER 9

We Do It to Ourselves

When we are little, our knowledge of the world is extremely limited. We grow up in a house in which we know our mother, our father, and our siblings. On the basis of limited knowledge and limited experience, we make decisions on how to think, feel and act. So far I have pointed out how we are programmed, but we also do it to ourselves. The decision age span in our culture is usually between five and thirteen or fourteen years, although there are exceptions. If we have been overstimulated when young or forced to use our brain very early, chances are that we are very bright and made decisions much earlier than five. Decisions we make as children are usually forgotten or are below the level of our awareness. Yet they form part of our programming. As adults, we act on early-life decisions without the awareness that we are doing so. We make decisions without having the ability to reason logically, as illustrated in the following examples.

Early Decision Illustrating
Syncretic (Blended) Perception

The client, aged thirty-two, never got angry at authority figures. Instead, she would be scared, become tongue-tied, shake, and then she would either be furious with herself or take her anger out on her children. She behaved this way with her husband, too, and later would feel burning resentment. In general, her relationship with her husband was very poor; she was withdrawing most of the time. She had taken an assertiveness training course, with little if any beneficial effect. Her goal, when she came into group therapy, was to be assertive. In regression analysis, she relived the following scene:

Marge: I'm furious! I'm two years old. I'm having a temper tantrum. I see red. My Mommy and Daddy are leaving me. Mommy is telling me, "It's all right. We won't be gone long. Mommy loves you." (Client lies quietly and then begins to shake.)

Shep: What's happening?

Marge: I'm scared. There was a fire next door a few days earlier, and a baby was killed. Her mother threw her out the window. I asked my mother about the baby next door, "How come the mother threw her out the window?" My mother told me that "her mother *loved* her, and had to throw her out the window because of the *fire*." I didn't know what fire was. I thought is was because she (the baby) got angry. I thought that if I got angry my mother would throw *me* out the window because she loved me. I didn't know what love meant. I *decided* never to get angry.

To the same two-year-old, seeing red, anger, and fire had the same meaning; that is, they were blended together. Anger mobilizes, and after this work, the client was able to get angry at her husband and tell him off. She reported when she finally did tell him off, he told her that he liked her this way and wished she had experienced her anger years ago. The relationship improved enormously, and she stopped getting angry and screaming at her children.

Early Decision Not to Have Fun

The client, aged thirty-eight, could laugh and have fun, but never around her family or her husband. Her husband had moved out of the house two years before and taken an apartment in the city. He had had an affair with a younger woman, but he had terminated the relationship six months before he left his wife. He would come home and spend every weekend with the family. The wife's goal was to get her husband to move back into the house permanently, and what she was currently working on in group therapy was having fun with her husband and family. In regression she reported the following:

Jenny: I'm having fun. I'm two years old. I'm in a chicken coop. (Client laughs.) They are pecking at me. They are so funny to watch. I see my mother. She is furious! She pulls me out of the coop. We are in the yard. She is hurting me, pulling at my hair, scratching me! She cuts my hair off!

Out of regression, Jenny reported: "I was covered with lice. She combed my hair with a very fine-tooth comb to get the lice out. I thought my mother was punishing me for having fun and laughing. I could never have fun or laugh when she was around."

Shep: How has this affected your life?
Jenny: I don't allow myself to laugh or have fun in the presence of my family or relatives. My husband is just like my mother, and I never laugh when he is around. All my life when my mother laughed or was having fun, I was furious with her because she could have fun and I couldn't.

Jenny gave herself permission to have fun with her family. As is often the case, the family then resisted having fun with Mom. Her husband, who had been in the habit of berating her for being such a sad sack, now resisted going out together and doing fun things. It was a full year after this particular piece of work that she was able to have some semblance of a happy, normal relationship with her family.

Early Decision to Be Careful

Very often the client will immediately tell the therapist exactly where he or she is headed and state his or her basic problem. We only delude ourselves that we keep secret our shortcomings.

We wear a mask and think that nobody can see us, but all the time we shout our what our problems are. If you tune in and *listen* carefully to what other people say, you will learn a lot from what they say. For example, Grace Wilson, my co-therapist, and I were talking to a trainee about a research project. I told him that I would outline a research project and bring in a suggestion. He said, "That would be great. Bring it in and we will kick it around." Grace looked at me and I looked at her. Sure enough, I brought in the suggestion, and he proceeded to kick it around for a year and a half.

In the following clinical case, we will outline a decision to be careful, arrived at via dream work.* Later I will detail techniques so that you may work with your own dreams.

Josie: I would like to *explore carefully* my dream before I make any decisions.

Shep: What is your dream?

Josie: There are four Christmas trees in my yard, and I see that one of them was blown over and uprooted after a storm. At the same time I thought somebody knocked it over.

Shep: What is going on in your current life that ties into this?

Josie: Well, I just landscaped my property and planted some trees, and I was *very careful* about how the job was done.

Shep: Be one of the trees in the dream and tell me how old you are.

Josie: About four years old. I got knocked down.

Shep: Stay with the feeling of "knocked down," let a scene come to you, don't think. What happened in real life when you were four? Who knocked you down?

Josie: What flashed in my mind is not that I got knocked down but my brother was chasing me into the kitchen once, and I knocked a cup off the table. He was in his bare feet, and he stepped on the cup and got a severe cut. His toe almost got cut off.

*S. Gellert, "How to Reach Early Scenes and Decisions by Dream Work," *Transactional Analysis Journal*, (October 1974)

Shep:	Close your eyes, relax, and stay with the scene. You are four years old, and your brother almost got his toe cut off. What is happening?
Josie:	My parents are screaming at me. They say I'm a wild Indian. I'm going to kill somebody, running around.
Shep:	So what did you decide?
Josie:	I decided to be *careful*, not to be spontaneous.
Shep:	So you're still living that out. Your goal was to *explore* your dreams *carefully* before making decisions.
Josie:	That's true. I've always been careful and organized and planned my life. I always cover my flanks and prepare for contingencies. That particular scene of us running through the kitchen has often come through my mind over the years, but I never connected it to my lack of spontaneity.

After reliving this scene, Josie decided that she could be spontaneous and not be so organized. She had been a staff executive with a large corporation, took early retirement, and is now in business for herself.

The child decision not to feel or not to show feelings is a common one. The following cases are just a few examples.

Early Decision Not to Express Feelings (1)

Shep:	What do you want for a goal?
Fanny:	I would like to express my feelings. In my current life I don't express my feelings to people. I have a dream.
Shep:	Tell me your dream.
Fanny:	I am in a carnival booth, and there is a little nine-year-old boy with a cap on his head. His mother is spraying stuff around him. It smells horrible . . . I tell her she shouldn't spray that stuff around; it will stunt his growth. Then the little boy takes off his cap and horrible bugs crawl and fly out of his head . . . ugh. I scream and run away, and then I wake up, feeling terrified.
Shep:	Get the feeling; stay with it. Relive that dream. When you get the feeling, just stay with it and keep breathing. When did you have that feeling when you

were nine years old and someone was spraying stuff around. Let the scene come to you. Don't think.

Fanny: We had just moved to a horrible apartment that had roaches. I was disgusted by them. Ech. I was lying in my bed and a roach crawled on my leg. I sat up and decided not to scream because it was the middle of the night. If I screamed and woke them up, my mother would have been angry and upset, and when they saw it was just a bug, they would have laughed at me. So I decided not to express my feelings.

Shep: How does this decision tie into your current life?

Fanny: I am not expressing my fear and anger. I think sometimes I am not even aware of my feelings.

Shep: If you will, go around the group and tell us how you'll be different.

Fanny: I will be aware of my fear and anger. I will express them if I choose to. I will not be afraid that people will get angry and upset, or angry and laugh at me.

Evidently, there had been previous incidents where Fanny got angry or scared and her parents would get angry and laugh at her; so she already knew that when the roach was on her leg, she should not waken her parents.

We did not get to that earlier scene. What we had was the childhood decision based on earlier experiences. But when I was working with the same client about three months later, she reached an earlier scene. It turned out that the decision not to express her feelings was part of a major message "not to tell, or you will be abandoned." The following is edited from the tape.

Fanny relives a scene in which she is four years old and is crying hysterically. She is at a summer resort, and her father leaves her to go to work for the week in the city. She feels he is leaving her for good. She often talks about this scene and connects it with a feeling of sadness. Fanny had had years of psychoanalysis in which she would lie on the couch and feel sad and talk about the scene. Now, rather than talk about it, she relaxes, breathes deeply, and relives the scene.

Fanny: Dad, don't leave me (cries hysterically for several minutes).

Shep: He did leave you, so what did you decide?

Fanny: I decided not to trust men. (This is the same "deci-
        sion" Fanny always reaches.)

Shep: You thought he left for good, because of something
        that happened earlier. Just stay with the breathing.
        What happened earlier?

Fanny: (Starts to laugh and giggle. Laughs and laughs.)

Shep: What's going on? Keep in touch.

Fanny: I'm in bed with my daddy, he's tickling me. (Laughs,
        then starts to cry and scream) Daddy, you hurt me.
        (Fanny continues to cry and writhe in pain, with her
        legs drawn up.)

After the emotional discharge, Fanny reported that her
father had molested her and told her not to tell anyone or he
would go away and never come back. She didn't tell, but when
he left for the week to go back to work, she thought he was leaving for good because he *thought* she had told. Her decision was
not to tell. She reported that her father had been sent to jail
when she was eight years old for molesting her girlfriend,
another eight-year-old.

The fact that Fanny was now expressing her feelings and her
thoughts brought up the early feeling scene and the decision not
to tell. But *Fanny had made the behavior change first*, before
understanding or analysis. After reliving the scene, she also
reported a great change in her body. She had relaxed her back
and leg muscles and the muscles in her genital area, that she
now lubricated freely during sex. Prior to this, she had only had
orgasms through manipulation or oral stimulation, but never
during penetration. Now she had vaginal orgasms during inter-
course.

Early Decision Not to Express Feelings (2)

Shep: Tell me your dream.

Mary: I'm riding on the outside of a steam engine going
        some place in the country, and I feel great.

Shep: What's going on in your current life that you're feel-
        ing great about?

Mary: I'm feeling great when I'm with my boyfriend and we

go out. I have been a spinster most of my life, and now I have this guy who is really swell to me. He's kind and I'm really enjoying life. And we're thinking of getting married.

Shep: Be you on the train and get that great feeling. How old are you?

Mary: I am very young, maybe four.

Shep: Stay there on the train with that great feeling and let a scene come to you when you felt that great and maybe you were four years old. Just keep your eyes closed, breathe, and relax. Let a scene come to you when you were feeling that great. Maybe you were going some place.

Mary: I've got the scene. I'm on a train and it's taking me to my music teacher's house.

Shep: Stay on the train. What happened to you when you were at the music teacher's house?

Mary: (Starts to shake) My parents went away for a weekend and left me there, and Herbert, my music teacher's husband, told me if I didn't behave I would be in the doghouse, and I was scared. I thought he meant he would chain me up in the doghouse.

Shep: What did you do?

Mary: I waited for my parents to come back, and I ran to them crying, and I told them I was scared of Herbert and what he said. They laughed at me.

Shep: So what did you decide?

Mary: I decided not to tell them how I felt any more.

Shep: How did you feel?

Mary: Angry and put down.

Shep: How does this tie in with your current life situation?

Mary: Now I'm still feeling angry and put down and not telling my boyfriend how I feel about his daughter. She is close to my age, and she keeps putting me down, and I don't tell him about it.

Childhood decisions are not logical in the adult sense, and out of our awareness we act on them without benefit of adult logic.

Mary was scared that her boyfriend's daughter would put her in the doghouse because of her relationship with her boyfriend. When she brought this up in the open and discussed it with her boyfriend, they cleared up the situation. Mary and her boyfriend are now happily married.

Early Decision Not to Tell

The client was the head nurse in a county facility for retarded children and reported that she was terrified of her new "tutor," who was an outside consultant psychiatrist hired to advise her department. He wasn't doing his job, and she was scared but determined not to quit.

Shep: When you were little, when did you have that scared feeling the first time?

Flo: We had a maid when I was four years old. My mother was sick, and I told my father I didn't like the maid, and he said I should be a good girl; we needed the maid or else my mother would die. I felt scared and put down. (This did not explain nor account for the here-and-now situation.)

Shep: What did the maid do so that you didn't like her?

Flo: She took me some place she wasn't supposed to.

Shep: (Key intervention)* Something happened, the maid was mean to you—or something happened. Lie down and relax (relaxation techniques) and tell me what happened.

Flo: (Shaking) Oh! I've got it. She took me to a house where she met another woman. The other woman was supposed to have stolen something, but she didn't have it. So, they yelled at each other. Then a man came in and he hit the other woman again and again. The maid took me home. She told me if I ever told anyone she would kill me. I was scared.

Shep: You never told anyone?

Flo: Never . . . come to think of it, my father later fired her for stealing.

*S. Gellert, "Key Scenes," *Transactional Analysis Journal*, (April 1976).

Shep: How does this tie into the here and now?

Flo: This psychiatrist is supposed to be taking care of my department, and he is not doing his job. I should report him to the hospital administrator.

This session was followed by work that involved her father and the maid and resulted in the redecision that "I can tell without being terrified that I will be killed" and "I can stand up for myself without being scared I will be put down."

Flo stayed on the job and wrote a report to the hospital administrator that the psychiatrist was not doing his job. She stood up for what she believed in and produced any number of changes in the facility where she was working. (This will sound odd, but one of the major things she did was have the mirrors lowered so that the children could see themselves. The mirrors in the washrooms were placed for the adults and not for the children. Little things like this sound picayune. However, for a little child who is in an institution, the small things mean a great deal.)

Early Decision Not to Feel Frightened and to Substitute Anger

Another client said he wanted to get rid of his anger. He had had five years of therapy with a prominent "feeling" therapist.

Shep: How do you expect to get rid of your anger?

Bob: I'll lie on the mat and have a temper tantrum.

Shep: Ever done that before?

Bob: Yes, thirty or forty times.

Shep: Change anything?

Bob: I felt better afterward.

Shep: For how long?

Bob: (Long pause) I keep making myself angry, all my life I've been angry. I want to stop being angry.

Shep: How do you make yourself angry?

Bob: I make myself angry by being stupid, finding fault with everybody—the government, my boss, the elevator operator, the receptionist, you know.

Shep: What do you want to change?

Bob: I want to stop making myself angry.

Shep: Get the feeling of anger. When did you have that feeling when you were little?

Bob: (Shakes and reports that he is four years old. He is with his sister and a girl cousin, both nine years old.)

Shep: What is happening?

Bob: My cousin has my arms pinned, my sister is twisting my foot. I'm scared they will kill me. (Client shakes.)

Shep: And then what happens?

Bob: I give up. (Client cries.) Don't hurt me. I give up, I'll behave.

Shep: And then what happens?

Bob: (Crying) They leave me alone. I'm all alone. (Client opens his eyes.)

Shep: So what did you decide?

Bob: They didn't want to play with me. I guess I was a pest. I decided to stay alone. Yeah, it was better to be angry and alone than to get hurt by them.

Shep: How has this affected your life?

Bob: I'm still alone. I don't approach women.

Bob had spent a lifetime getting himself angry at women and blocking his scare feelings. Once he was aware that he was scared of women, he regularly told himself that all women are not his sister and he is no longer four years old.

Another client, aged forty-two, when asked if she could tell her husband how she felt, replied:*

Linda: I can't (in a child's voice).

Shep: What are you feeling?

Linda: Sad.

Shep: Stay with that sad feeling. Repeat, "I can't."

Linda: I can't, I can't, I can't.

Shep: Make a sentence, "I can't . . ."

Linda: I can't do anything. I can't do anything right. (Client begins to cry.)

Shep: How old do you feel?

Linda: Around three.

*Not too many early scenes and decisions are this easy to get at.

Shep: What happened when you were three? Stay with the feeling.

Linda: (Client is regressed and reports:) When I was real little, I used to fart in the house, and my parents thought it was cute. When I was three years old, I was a flower girl at my sister's wedding, and I was so happy, and I farted when I was up at the alter. When we got home, my father was very angry and disgusted with me and told me I *never did anything right.*

Shep: What did you decide?

Linda: I decided I couldn't do anything right.

Shep: How are you symbolically stinking up the atmosphere in the here and now?

Linda: I play stupid, helpless, and I do everything wrong.

Shep: Sounds like you control everybody with your helplessness.

Linda: I never thought of it that way.

Shep: What do you want to start doing right?

Linda then set goals to do fun things with her family and her husband, and stop playing helpless and stupid. She has been very successful and also has lost thirty pounds. It is not unusual for clients to make changes in areas of their lives other than the area for which they are in group therapy.

Spontaneous Decisions

In the absence of parental programming, decisions can occur spontaneously because of the limited intelligence of the young child or the child's *misunderstanding* or the parent's *words* or *behavior*. Decisions may also be made in response to chance occurrences in the environment, such as bee stings, childhood diseases, falls, accidents, or a shack falling on the child. The following examples illustrate all three of these possibilities.

• The client, aged forty-five, was very quiet, spoke in a low voice, and didn't move about very much. He thought this was his nature. In working through early scenes, however, he was seen as a very active child. The client did not see his quietness as a problem, nor did the group. However, on a hunch:

Shep: When did you decide to be so quiet?

George: (After a long pause) I was eight years old. I was in an auto accident, and my left arm was almost severed from my body. The doctor told me not to move around and to be quiet, or I would die. I decided I'd better be quiet.

• Another client, aged twenty-four, was very cautious. He stopped himself from learning how to ride a two-wheel bicycle, engaging in sports, and the like. He reported the following scene:

Steve: I am six or seven years old. We moved into a new house, and I went exploring in the woods in back of the house. I walked into a wasp's nest. They are all over me! I run to my father, who brushes them off. I hurt! I decide I'd better be careful and not take any chances.

•Steve's sister, aged twenty-two, is "not assertive" with men. In regression analysis, she recalls the following scene.

Ellen: I see my brother. I'm four years old. My father is hitting him. I yell, "Daddy, don't hit him! He didn't do anything! He is covered with wasps!" My father keeps hitting him. I decide I'd better do what my father wants me to do.

The father reported that he remembered the incident well. He did not hit his son; he was terrified because he saw the boy covered with wasps for the second time in two hours and had vigorously brushed them off. He had later scoured the woods and destroyed three nests in back of his house.

There are various ways of reaching the early scene and decisions. Early experiences are organized in our minds on the basis of their emotional content. By staying with the feeling and allowing ourselves to relax, an early scene will very often come to us. The process of thinking about or talking about—for example, in free association—interferes with the reliving and re-experiencing of early scenes.

It should be noted that the examples I cite in this chapter do not reflect the fact that the people in group have been working on changing their behavior for quite some time. The early scene usually comes *after* a person has set a goal and has taken steps toward changing on a behavioral level.

For the purpose of writing, I have separated imprints, introjects, and decisions. Every one of us has made dozens of early childhood decisions; if we are fortunate, most of them have not limited our happiness. In real life the process is not that simple, and I am including the following clinical case, edited from tapes, that illustrates introject and decisions.

Early Decision Not to Feel Angry and Not to Feel Scared ("Scared" Equals "Crazy")

• Glenda, a forty-two-year-old woman, had scarlet fever at the age of three and was hospitalized. During the illness she had periods of delirium from the high fever, and for four months she could not walk. Glenda had a history of chronic back disorders.

Shep: What is it you want?

Glenda: I want to get rid of the pain in my neck and back muscles. I think it's anger.

Shep: Relax (relaxation procedures and exercises) and breathe deeply. Be aware of your breathing, and then fantasize you are very young, the age you were when you first decided to tighten your muscles. Imagine you are getting very small, very small. See yourself on a television screen in your mind, getting smaller and smaller. When you are very small and very young, swallow yourself and go down into your stomach and then move through your body and look at those muscles that hurt. Keep in touch and let me know where you are.*

Glenda: I'm in my back.

Shep: What does it look like?

Glenda: It's a different kind of anger from the neck muscles.

Shep: Beat and kick the pillows and get the anger out.

Glenda: (Beats and kicks the pillows until exhausted.)

Shep: Keep breathing and let a scene come to you.

Glenda: (Whispers) My back, my back (louder), it's not

---

*This is a Gestalt therapy fantasy technique.

broken (very loud) . . . it's whole. It isn't broken (very loud). My back isn't broken. I can stand, I can walk, I can walk.

Shep: How old are you?

Glenda: I was three years old and I was so frightened, so frightened (voice and body shake, fear comes out). When I came home from the hospital, my father told me I couldn't walk and I believed him. I believed him.

Shep: What happened when you were three years old?

Glenda: I was crazy. I felt animals all over me.

Shep: What kind of animals?

Glenda: Tigers, and they were eating me, and I really saw them, and I was frightened and I was crazy.

Shep: Who told you you were crazy?

Glenda: I did. (Glenda reported months later that she vividly recalled telling herself that she was crazy. To a three-year-old, being crazy, whatever that meant, was better than being eaten by tigers.)

Shep: What did you say?

Glenda: (Voice loud, sarcastic and harsh—an adult voice) "You can't have animals eating you. You're crazy." (introject).

Shep: Who said that?

Glenda: My mother. I had a fever, and I was delirious, and I was frightened. I told my mother the animals were eating me, and she told me I was crazy.

Shep: What is it you want to tell your mother?

Glenda: Leave me alone. (Kicks pillows) Leave me alone, I am not crazy. (Voice loud and angry) I am me. I am angry, I am angry. (Tantrum, anger comes out, and client is now exhausted.)

Since the time she was three, Glenda, instead of feeling her anger, tightened her neck and back muscles, giving herself pain. In the original scene her mother told her she was crazy. When her mother's introjected voice came out, this was like an electrode telling her she was crazy. Glenda could not get angry at her mother when she was very young and could not get angry at authority figures when she was older.

In the dream work that follows, one year later, Glenda is

now forty-three years old. The scene she recalls is when she was five. Her mother had gone out and told her to stay in the house. A fourteen-year-old boy scared her when he knocked on her door and told her he was the big, bad wolf. She was terrified and ran out of the house. For Glenda to feel scared meant that she thought she was crazy. At the age of thirty-nine, Glenda was scared by the fact that her daughter was on drugs and she thought she, Glenda, was going crazy.

Shep: Tell me your dream.
Glenda: I am a young girl, four or five years old, and I am standing by a lake or pond. There is a witch in a rowboat in the pond with a calico cat in her hand, and I am standing on the shore. I holler and cry "Please don't drown the cat," but I couldn't rescue the cat because I was afraid of drowning. So I let the cat die.
Shep: When did you dream this?
Glenda: I dreamed it when I was five years old, and I just remembered it a couple of weeks ago.
Shep: What is going on in your current life where you feel helpless?
Glenda: I feel helpless in my marriage.
Shep: Get the feeling from the dream. What is going on when you are five years old?
Glenda: I feel cold, shaky, quivering in my stomach. I am reminded of the rain. It is raining and it's dark. Oh, I remember now. I ran out of the house because I was scared by a boy, and I ran down the street to a neighbor's hose where my mother was, and she made me go home.* I am walking up the hill, and she keeps throwing me down on the ground and hitting me with a stick. She hits me until I fall down, and then she picks me up and keeps hitting me. I am shaking. I am cold and scared. My knees are shaking.
Shep: What is your mother saying to you?
Glenda: (Harsh adult voice) "You are bad. You are bad. You are crazy. There is nothing to be afraid of."

*Not unusual, the client goes in and out of regression. The change in tense "I ran" indicates she is out of regression and reporting. These shifts are accompanied by voice changes.

Shep: What did you decide?

Glenda: I decided that I must be crazy when I feel scared
          because there is nothing to be scared about.

Shep: What do you want to say to your mother?

Glenda: (Young voice) "I am not crazy. I feel scared. The big
          bad wolf was at the back door, and he told me if I
          didn't let him in he would blow my house down so I
          ran." (Shift to mature voice) My mother hated me
          when I was sick and scared.

Shep: So what did you decide?

Glenda: If I felt scared, not to show it, not to let her know I
          was scared. That if I was scared I must be crazy.

Shep: What are you aware of now?

Glenda: I just want to say that I am aware that being scared
          doesn't make me crazy. When I became frightened, I
          always felt there was something wrong with me if I
          was frightened.

Shep: Put your mother on the chair and tell her, "Mom,
          I'm forty-three years old" and make up some
          sentences.

Glenda: Mom, I am forty-three years old, and I am not going
          to take on your crazy. I am going to feel scared when
          I'm scared and not think I'm crazy because I'm
          frightened. I will feel it and show it.

Shep: What does your mother say?

Glenda: (Harsh voice) "You can't blame me for the way you
          feel."

Shep: What do you say to her?

Glenda: "You're right. I think I will go now." (Glenda sits
          quietly and gradually gets very excited.) "Gee, all
          right, sure."

Shep: Sure what.

Glenda: Oh sure, a couple of years ago when I went to the
          counselor, that's when I had the psychotic episode
          when I was so frightened and so scared and that's
          when it really came out.

Shep: What came out?

Glenda: The scare, just scare. Fear that my daughter was go-
          ing to die from taking drugs, fear that . . . I mean it

was overexaggerated because I hadn't allowed myself to feel scare, and all the time I was frightened. I kept holding it back and holding it back and not saying anything to my husband about how frightened I was, and when I did, he got angry and started screaming at me and telling me I was crazy.

Shep: Oh wow.

Glenda: And I wasn't crazy.

Shep: So he ran the same scene over.

Glenda: The same thing that my mother ran. I married my mother.

Early Decision Not to Feel Happy

When I was three and a half, I was let out of the apartment each morning to play and was told to be back for lunch at noon. The little boy next door, a three-year-old, and I crossed the street, which was forbidden, and went to play in a vacant lot between two apartment buildings. We had a great time there pulling up weeds and doing whatever else three-year-olds do. I had to go to the bathroom, and he had to go at the same time. It must have been around noon and he said, "Let's go home." I told him we didn't have to, we could pull down our pants and make (bowel movement) and wipe our rear ends with the leaves.

He agreed that this was a great idea, and we proceeded to do this. Having relieved ourselves, we then played until two-thirty. He told me I was a genius. Neither of us knew what that meant, but the admiration in his voice told me that it was the highest form of a compliment—the first positive recognition from my peer group—this was an accolade! I was floating on clouds when I went home at two-thirty.

When I got home, my mother had my father take me into the bedroom and beat me with a strap. They had been searching the neighborhood when I did not return at noon and had been scared. I relived this scene and felt the numbness in my fingers where the belt buckle hit me, and felt the burning in my legs as I ran around the room in a circle while my father stood in the center flailing me with the strap.

I *decided* then and there that *it was not safe to be happy.* At that age, I did not understand that my parents were scared. I saw them only as angry. I lived out this decision, not to be happy, until I was forty-six years old.

Remembering and *recalling*, however, are quite different from *reliving*. In reliving, the emotional part is felt and the scene is *reexperienced*.

At the age of forty-six, I changed my behavior and started to be good to myself and do things that made me happy. It wasn't until three years later, *after* I had developed the techniques for regression analysis, that the early scene came to me.

I changed without reliving the scene! Had I wanted to get the scene first, I might still be waiting! That it is possible and more productive to change behavior first frequently has to be explained to the client who wants to "find out why" first and change later.

Not All the Decisions the Child Makes are Bad

• I had a client whose family pressures were to "be sick." Her mother constantly took her to the doctor, and her younger sister spent her life in and out of mental institutions. The client recalled that at the age of five, her mother dragged her to the doctor's office. The doctor, instead of comforting and being kind, probably was angry at the mother for constantly dragging the kids in. He was nasty to the client. She remembers making the decision then that she "would not be sick." She spent her life not being sick. This was a very fortunate decision compared with that of her sister. The client was in group therapy because she felt unappreciated. Part of the decision to be strong was not to allow herself to be nurtured or comforted, so she was doing everything for everybody. After she relived the scene, she gave herself permission to be weak and to have people do things for her. In shorthand lingo, she was a programmed giver.

•Another client relived a scene when he was about six and was bitten in the rear end by a dog. After this experience he decided to be cautious. Even though he ran around in the country with a bunch of kids who were always doing wild things—one of his friends fell off a mountain and was killed; another wrecked a car and was killed—he behaved wildly in a very cautious way. His decision to be cautious saved his life several times. This was a mixed blessing, because the decision also kept him locked into an unhappy marriage. Shortly thereafter he was able to come to an amiable financial settlement with his wife (he didn't get bit in the hip pocket).

The point I make is that even if a decision is a good one, it limits our spontaneity and our options. This client had been backing out of his marriage for eight years. Some of us have been backing out of marriages for twenty years.

Some therapists have made a religion of primal therapy, but deeper and deeper is not always better and better. Using regression analysis, I have had clients relive birth scenes and have often found them to be nontherapeutic. The client is usually avoiding a traumatic scene that occurred at the age of two or three, and reliving the birth scene is less scary for him or her.

One of the strangest scenes in my experience relates to a client who reported, "I see myself being lifted out of my mother's stomach."* He called his mother and asked if his was a Cesarean birth. She told him it was, and he had never known it. Observing such scenes are fascinating for the therapist, but nontherapeutic for the client!

Clients who are reliving birth scenes change the contours of their face; their chin may disappear, their features and voice may change. In regression, the face and feet are far more flexible than I would ever have imagined possible for grown-ups.

If people do not have a set goal, it is not unusual for them to drift all over and get scenes that really have no obvious meaning or therapeutic impact. An extremely common occurrence is for people to relive childhood diseases. It seems these leave a very heavy memory trace. Fortunately, my co-therapist has been an orthopedic nurse, has worked with children, and is familiar with most of the childhood diseases, so that we can readily identify the disease the client is reliving and then, when he or she is out of the regression, check it out. Those clients who had no memory but whose parents were living checked it out with their parents. Over and over the early-scene material has been validated.

---

*This seems to be not unlike the perceptual experiences reported by people who have died and come back to life.

One of the funniest early scenes was with a client who was lying on the mat regressing and who reported a scene where she saw herself the age of three and a half in her neighbor's apartment. The neighbor used to be her baby-sitter. She saw the living room, the sunlight streaming through the window, and she was sitting there with a book. About that time, in the regression her stomach disappeared; that is to say, her stomach drew in until, from a side view, it went from about eight inches thick to about four inches thick. She started to burp, and her stomach grumbled, and she reported a feeling of terrible cramps in her stomach. I asked her, "What's going on?" and she told me she was "eating the book." After she was out of the regression, she reported that she ate the whole book, page by page, because it tasted so good. She took each page, chewed it up and swallowed it; then, of course, she had terrible cramps. This scene had absolutely no effect on her life and had nothing to do with anything we were working on.

We store all experiences in our minds, vast computer banks of memories, where they remain—the good, the bad, and the indifferent—most of them way below the level of our awareness. We also have a dual recording: one track is abstract-symbolic, the other contains our actual feelings and thoughts and decisions at the time of the experience.

Feelings are primitive thoughts or, putting it another way feelings are our awareness of internal experience. Feelings are biological, not logical. Our language to describe internal and sensory experience is very limted, and being seemingly rational creatures, we keep trying to explain feelings logically. In the next chapter I will fall into this trap. Feel free to disagree.

CHAPTER 10

Feelings

We are all born with biologically programmed feelings. The newborn infant, when dropped, will exhibit a startled, scared reaction; if prevented from moving, the infant will exhibit a temper tantrum and exhibit rage; if not fed when hungry or if hurt, the infant will cry with sadness or scream with pain.

In lower animals and in humans, the simplest response is the reflex. In higher animals, the emotions correspond to primitive thoughts: anger equals attack; scare equals run. We human beings can have a whole variety of reflex responses. If a ball is thrown at us, we duck (reflex); if we get a notice to appear before the Internal Revenue Service, we feel scared. However, in our "civilized" society, very often emotions are not useful for problem solving. As contrasted with primitive times, when man lived largely by his senses and basic biological emotions.

Imagine back to one hundred thousand years ago. Man then had to be constantly in touch with the environment, with the here and now. There was not much time for daydreaming, thinking about the past or the future. The major problem facing them was "do we eat today" or "will we be eaten today." If they got through the day successfully and ate (survival of the self), the next item on the agenda was reproduction (survival of the species).

Consider that a prehistoric man walking alone one hundred thousand years ago hears a rustle, rustle in the bushes—something moving. He stands erect so he can see better, straightens his head, and starts processing with his sense of smell and all his other senses. If he smells a rabbit (in those days, our sense of smell hadn't been bred out of us), he will turn his excitement into motion toward it. If he gets the rabbit, he will turn his excitement into a feeling of gladness. And if he doesn't get it he will turn his excitement into sadness.

Now suppose another creature blocks him from getting the rabbit. If the creature is smaller than he, he picks up a rock and smashes it in the head; if it's bigger than he, he backs off. If it's an object that blocks him and there's nothing he can do about it, he turns his excitement into anger. *Anger is wanting somebody or something to change its behavior.* Don't take my word for it. The next one hundred thousand times you get angry, pay attention to yourself and see if you aren't making yourself angry by wanting something or someone to change its behavior.

Imagine that for the man in our discussion the obstacle is insurmountable and prevents him from catching the rabbit. He will turn his excitement into a mixed emotion, frustration. He will be sad because he didn't get what he wanted; angry because he wanted the object to change its behavior; and possibly scared because he is going to starve. Anger and frustration are excitement that we are unable to discharge. Our man would not stay angry or frustrated for very long. He would get back into his senses and proceed with living, because his routine is simple and he has not been trained to save up and not to display his feelings.

Now consider another case. Our prehistoric man hears a rustle, rustle, rustle, takes a sniff, and smells a saber-toothed tiger. Again, he turns his excitement into motion, "feet get going." If he gets away, he turns his excitement into gladness. If he is not successful, he doesn't have any excitement to do anything about.

Suppose something stops him and he can't run away. He then turns his excitement into scare, and he will biologically freeze. The reason he freezes is because there is less chance of being noticed if he stays motionless. He sucks in his gut, raises his shoulders, tightens his anal sphincter, and closes down his whole breathing system. Pure terror! Scare is wanting to get away from somebody or something and not being able to do so. These are basic biological feelings: excitement, glad/sad, anger/scare.

Consider the following diagram. The column represents body excitement, which may be expressed as gladness, fright, sadness, or anger, and which, if the emotion is suppressed, results in anxiety at one end of the spectrum and depression at the other. Body excitement is determined by the amount of oxygen we take in. If we breathe shallowly and slowly, we lower the level of excitement; if we breathe rapidly and deeply, we raise it. If we suppress our excitement by lowering our breathing level, by not taking in much air, by tightening our muscle systems to burn energy as in isometric exercises, we can turn our excitement into depression. If we increase our breathing (hyperventilate) but are programmed not to feel excited or sad (or some other appropriate feelings), we can turn our excitement into anxiety.

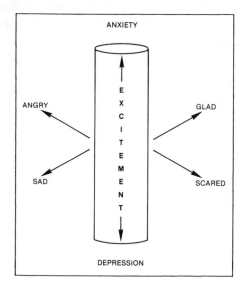

Figure 3
Depression

Programmed Feelings

Programmed feelings are natural feelings we give ourselves that we were trained to feel when we were young, with *parental indulgence*; they are substitute feelings. So instead of feeling scared, we feel angry; instead of feeling sad, we feel scared; instead of feeling happy, we feel anxious; instead of feeling excited, we feel depressed. Some of us are trained not to feel much at all (in the medical model, the extreme is labeled the schizoid character).

One client tells of growing up in a house where none of the children was allowed to show anger. If she raised her voice or expressed anger, she was told not to act crazy. Her father was often angry at her mother; he yelled and threw things. Mom always would cry or look sad (when she was really furious at him). The client grew up and substituted a sad feeling whenever she was angry.

In another family, the sad feeling was not allowed. When the family pet died, the client was told not to be silly when she cried over the loss. "We'll buy you another dog, it's only an animal." The parent's response to her sadness was anger; the client began substituting anger for sad.

Conditioned Response

Pavlov took some dogs into a lab, then rang a bell and fed them. He learned that when the bell rang, the dogs started to salivate, even before food was available. You may have heard the story about Pavlov's dogs. A new dog was sent to Pavlov's laboratory. The new dog asked the old dog, "What's it like here?" The old dog answered, "It's great. They have an idiot in a white jacket thoroughly trained, and at the ring of a bell, he brings us food." The conditioned response operates like this: We can be conditioned to give ourselves certain feelings, and the feelings are real, even when the stimulus is no longer there.

When I am little and Daddy yells at me and hits me, I hurt. Fifty years later if I say, "So and so hurt me," and though they did not physically abuse me, they raised their voice or gave me a look or said something, or put me down, and "I hurt," then I am running a conditioned response. The very words "put down," incidentally, indicate that the infant may have been "put down" in his crib, that is, abandoned. Instead of blaming the other person, I would do well to recondition myself so that I no longer feel the way I did when I was two years old.

The conditioning can be extremely subtle. For example, the infant cries, the parents will come pick him or her up, so the infant learns that the way to get attention is by crying or being sad.

When the little girl baby becomes a little older, her parents may buy her a Pitiful Pearl doll or a Raggedy Ann doll and read her stories about sad little girls who in the end find Prince Charming. We learn to be sad and spend our life waiting for Prince Charming, or our parents may ignore us when we cry, so we learn that crying doesn't work as it did when we were infants, and substitute some other feelings.

Attributions (Curses)

We may be told we have a terrible temper like Uncle Charlie's or we're just like Uncle Charlie (who has a terrible temper). Mommy and Daddy may smile when we have a temper tantrum—positive reinforcement.

Role Model

The parents may role-model an angry person. They may yell at us, "Don't you get angry," (the message being nonverbal), "To be an adult means being angry like me," or they may pick us up and shake us in a homicidal rage, saying "Don't you be angry." Then we have our options. We can either grow up homicidal maniacs or go the other way and decide it's not safe to feel our anger.

Decisions

In early childhood we may decide what's safe to feel and what isn't safe to feel. We then forget that we made the decisions and live our lives on the basis of how we were programmed and how we programmed ourselves. We give ourselves bad feelings *outside* our awareness, while all the time, *in our awareness*, thinking we don't want to feel bad.

There's a time when *we have control* of our feelings. When we are young, *we turn them off* and *turn them on*. We've all seen children three, four, or five years old out playing. One may fall and be hurt, and then stand up and look around. There's no Mommy. Does the child cry? No, he or she waits. An hour later, Mommy comes out. Immediately, the child turns on the water-works, "Mommy I fell down." She responds with a hug and a kiss, and the child "feels better."

We've also seen brother and sister playing nicely together until the parents come home. "She hit me." "He bit me." "She broke my toy." "He pulled my hair." Instant mayhem, looking for the parents to be the judge, pleading their case.

The parent asks, "Did you break the lampshade?" and the little kid starts to cry. Crying, children have learned, avoids the dreaded punishment. Or children learn the major cop-out words, "I'm sorry." "It was an accident."

A client reported that her seven-year-old son was a crybaby, and when he didn't get his own way, he would carry on for hours. One weekend he wanted to go camping, and she told him no. He started to cry buckets, and she looked at him and said, "Cut it! It won't work!" He immediately stopped crying, looked at her, smiled, and said, "Sometimes it does."

Mixed Emotions

As Pavolv's dogs salivate when somebody rings a bell, somebody in our lives pushes a button ringing an emotional bell and we feel _____. Conditioned responses often show up in mixed emotions, which may be a combination of biological feelings and programmed feelings. Many emotions are mixed: embarrassment, jealousy, worry, envy, and frustra-tion. Table 1 helps to clarify what I mean by part-biological and part-programmed feelings.

TABLE 1

Emotion	May Be Biological	May Be Programmed
Worry	Scare	Scare/Anger
Embarrassment	Happy	Scare
Envy	Anger	Sadness
Jealousy	Anger	Fear of Abandonment (Scare)
Frustration	Anger/Sad	Scare

In my experience, people are better able to "cure" themselves of feeling bad when they separate the components and deal with each individually. Someone may ring your bell, but you don't have to answer. The following examples illustrate how to deal with mixed emotions.

Embarrassment

• Laura was forty-five years old and had come into group therapy to overcome her shyness. She wore shapeless dresses, steel-rimmed glasses, and looked very unattractive. At social gatherings she was a wallflower and remained in the background.

Shep: Will you go around the room and ask for physical strokes?

Laura: I couldn't do that. I would be too embarrassed.

Shep: What was your most embarrassing experience?

Laura: During the war there was no elastic for underwear, and my underpants had a button. I was fifteen and walking home from school one day. The button broke, and my pants fell down around my legs. The boys laughed at me. I took the underpants off and put them in my purse.

Shep: If you will, for experiment, finish this sentence: "I was delighted my pants fell down because . . ."

Laura: Because I got a lot of attention.

Shep: Finish this sentence: "I was scared because . . ." (What would your parents say?)

Laura: Because I was afraid my mother would find out.

Shep: How do those parts fit?

Laura: They fit.

Shep: Will you take the risk of asking for physical strokes, even though it's scary?

Laura: Okay, I guess nothing bad will happen.

After this piece of work, Laura began taking more and more risks, and within six months had blossomed into a beautiful woman. She changed her hairstyle, wore makeup, and dressed attractively. She turned out to be a man killer and ran through about four men in three years until she found the one she liked enough to marry. Today she is happily married with two children.

Jealousy

- Jean: I get very jealous when I go out with my boyfriend and he talks to other women.

Shep: Will you say the same sentence, but instead of using the word "jealous," will you substitute, "I'm angry. I want him to change his behavior, and at the same time, am scared of being abandoned (or scared of losing him)?"

Jean: I'm angry at my boyfriend. I want him to change his behavior, and I am scared of losing him.

Shep: How does that fit?

Jean: It fits.

Shep: Will your anger help change his behavior?

Jean: No, I think he does it to get me angry.

Shep: What do you want to do about your anger?

Jean: I'll make a contract to stop making myself angry when he talks to other women.

Shep: Does scaring yourself help you keep your boyfriend?

Jean: No, it doesn't help.

Shep: What do you want to do about that?

Jean: I want to stop scaring myself about losing him.

Shep: Will you stop scaring yourself about losing him?

Jean: Yes.

Shep: How can you do that?

Jean: I can tell myself that just because he's talking to other women doesn't mean he's going to leave me, and that it's normal for him to talk to other people, which it is.

Jean kept her goal, or contract, and did not get jealous when her boyfriend talked to other women. He consequently escalated his behavior to the point that he would take her somewhere and then ignore her. It became evident to Jean that he was programmed to tease women and get them angry. She decided she didn't need to go through life with a fellow who liked to pull the wings off butterflies, and dumped him. She felt she was extremely lucky to have found this out in time, rather than marry him and spend a life being jealous and angry and worrying about losing him.

Worry

Pat: I worry about my son. I worry about my husband's job. I worry all the time.

Shep: When you were small, who showed you how to worry?

Pat: My mother.

Shep: Pick one scene when you had Mom very worried.

Pat: I had pneumonia when I was six years old and almost died. My mother worried about me. She often told me how worried she was.

Shep: Be Mom, and tell little Pat about the worry.

Pat: (Play-roles her mother.) "You are nothing but aggravation. All my life you've been one problem after another. When you were six years old, I stayed up day and night," etc. (Mom's voice is angry.)

Shep: How are you feeling, Mom?

Pat: (As Mom) "Resentful. She doesn't appreciate all I did for her."

Shep: Pick another scene when you had Mom worried.

Pat: I stayed out until 1:00 A.M. when I was sixteen. When I got home, there was some scene. Mom yelled at me. I had her worried sick.

Shep: Be Mom and yell at you.

Pat: "You rotten kid! You had me worried sick!"

Shep: How do you feel, Mom?

Pat: Angry.

Shep: How did you feel while you were waiting for your daughter?

Pat: Scared and resentful.

Shep: Instead of using the word "worried," will you substitute, "I am angry. I want that person to change his or her behavior, and I'm scared."

Pat: Yes, I'm angry at my son, and I'm scared he will flunk out of school.

Shep: Which do you want to work on first? Your anger or your scare?

Envy

Tom: I am always envious of people who have something I don't have, or who I imagine have something I don't have.

Shep: For experiment, will you say, "I'm angry. I want them to change their behavior, and at the same time, I'm feeling sorry for myself, when I see people who . . ."

Tom does this and reports "it fits."

Shep: Which do you want to work on first, your anger or your sadness (self-pity)?

Frustration

Frustration is the most difficult of the mixed emotions to cure yourself of, because in the attempt you may wind up frustrated. The first thing to ask yourself is, "How can I frustrate myself in getting rid of my frustration?" The following case may be helpful.

Herb: I'm frustrated in my job. I feel frustrated all the time. No matter what I do, it's not good enough. The boss is always criticizing me.

Shep: Okay, will you break that up into anger, sad, and scared, and make up sentences, "I am angry at my job because . . . I am sad because . . . and I am scared because . . ."

Herb: Okay, I am angry at my boss because I want him to change his behavior. I want him to love me. I want him to accept me. I want him to tell me I'm a good boy. (Laughs)

Shep: Your boss pays your salary?

Herb: Yeah.

Shep: So, how long are you going to make yourself angry because he doesn't love and accept you?

Herb: (Laughs) I can give that up now.

Shep: Go on with the sadness.

Herb: I am sad on the job because I'm not getting the recognition I want.

Shep: And?

Herb: Yeah. My boss is a critical person, and he never will give me recognition. It's just not in him.

Shep: Go on.

Herb: And I'm scared. I guess I'm scared I'll get fired.

Shep: What's the reality?

Herb: The reality is I'm a civil servant, and he'd have to stand on his head to get rid of me.

Shep: So, how do you frustrate yourself on the job?

Herb: Ah, I frustrate myself by wanting recognition and acceptance, which I'm not going to get from my boss.

Feeling Cycles

In addition to mixed emotions, feeling cycles also exist. Very common are anger/remorse, anger/guilt. We get angry and then are sorry we blew our stack, or we feel guilty. Feeling cycles can become quite complex. The repetitiveness of the feeling cycles will tell you if the feeling is a chance occurrence or a programmed pattern, and you will then have an opportunity to figure out how to break the pattern.

The following clinical case will detail one such pattern.

Sarah had been a beautiful child, and at the age of forty was a beautiful woman. When working in therapy, she would get scared; her chin would quiver; she looked about three years old; then she'd become confused and be unable to think. She would next begin to cry and feel sad; then she'd get angry and flail out at the therapist or the group. Later she would become angry at herself and kick herself for being stupid. This was a lifelong pattern.

Sarah was taught techniques for removing the scare, and after she had stopped scaring herself, she recalled that when she was three years old, her five-year-old brother cut himself severely. Her mother tried to stop the bleeding and screamed at Sarah, in *German*, to run outside and get a taxi to take them to the hospital. Sarah didn't understand *German*, since her parents usually spoke English. She stood scared, not moving, until her mother finally yelled in English. She ran out, but no taxi would stop for a three-year-old. She went back into the house and started to cry (if she cried, Mommy wouldn't punish her). The anger was added later, when she was older. In an argument with her husband, children, or others, she would feel scared, then confused. She'd feel as if she wasn't understood, and she would become sad and cry. Finally she'd get angry with people for not understanding, and afterward get angry at herself for "being stupid" and not making herself understood. At the age of forty, she would become a three-year-old in the presence of authority figures or her own children!

The therapeutic solution Sarah reached was to stop *trying* to think when she was scared, and to wait for the scare to pass. This minor change enabled Sarah to raise her self-esteem, improve her relations with her husband and children, and lead a happier life.

Programmed feelings are not really caused by here-and-now events. The only time we can be alive is in the here and now. We can't live in the past; we can't live in the future; we can only live now. Our memories of the past are distorted, selective. What will occur in the future is only our fantasy. Right now I can stay in the here: I can be with you in the here and now, I can be in touch with you, or I can leave the here and go there. I can talk about other things, other people, other places, and because I'm talking about them I am not with you. We don't have intimacy. And that is important, because intimacy is something we all want. I can leave you by withdrawing in space, going somewhere else, watching television, or leaving the now by thinking of the past or the future. The here and now is such an important concept because I can't have bad feelings in the present unless something is currently happening.

"If Only"

I can leave the here and now and give myself bad feelings by going into the past and playing "if only." My mother was an expert at giving herself bad feelings—"black belt tenth degree"; she would sit in the kitchen, look out the window, and tears would come to her eyes. I would say, "What's the matter, Ma?" She would say, with a big sigh, "I was thinking of my grandfather." My mother's grandfather died when he was ninety-eight. He was swimming off Rockaway Beach when he had an appendicitis attack. At the hospital, it was misdiagnosed as pneumonia. His appendix burst and he died. For years, any time we drove by that hospital, Mom would look and say (angrily), "There is where they killed my grandfather." What Mom was doing was playing a game of "if only" in order to feel sad or angry.

Some of us are experts at playing "what if," going into the future to get bad feelings.

"What If"

If I'm driving a car, the here and now is I'm driving a car. It's a beautiful day. There are trees, people, but instead of being alive at the moment, I can think about next week, "I'll meet Joe . . . I'll say . . . he'll contradict me . . . I'll say," and now I'm angry. I just gave myself a bad feeling. An easy way to recognize programmed feelings is that they're the bad feelings we give ourselves when we're all alone. One of the hardest things in therapy is to get people out of the blaming position and to accept the fact that they are responsible for their own feelings, that we give ourselves bad feelings. Others may ring the bell or push the buttons, but we don't have to answer, even though we may have salivated or trembled or gone into a rage at that bell for thirty or more years.

What are here-and-now bad feelings? If somebody steps on my toe, my toe hurts. If I'm standing on a street corner waiting for a bus for twenty minutes, and the bus comes and goes by without stopping, what I'll feel is anger. That's a here-and-now anger. If I stay angry for five, ten minutes, that's understandable. If, on the other hand, I throw rocks at the bus and go home and start writing letters to the bus company, or if I go to the top of a high building and start shooting a gun at buses, then believe me, it's not a here-and-now feeling. If I get something and I feel glad, that's here and now. If I don't get it and I feel sad, that's here and now.

Playing Without a Full Deck—"Don't Feels"

When we're born, we start life with a full deck, fifty-two cards, four suits of thirteen cards each. Then we're programmed, and some of the cards are pulled out. These are the "don't feel" programs. So now we're playing without a full deck. For example, I was programmed to feel anger at males, but never at females. So I was missing the anger at women; as a result, as an adult I dumped all my anger on my son, not on my wife or my daughter. Some people are programmed not to feel angry, sad, or glad, but just feel scared. So they find a lot of ways to make themselves feel scared.

When we were young, two, three, or four years old, we couldn't hide our emotions. We hadn't learned how yet. We've all seen little children sneak into the house. They come in the door and hug the wall as they try to get to their room. Mom and Dad ask, "What did you do?" They look up and think, "How did they know?" Children have not learned to hide their feelings. We reach a point at which we learn to hide our feelings by tightening our back muscles, raising our blood pressure, giving ourselves asthma attacks, ulcers, arthritis, colitis, bursitis, lower back pains, neck pains, headaches, and a lot of psychosomatic illnesses—going through life keeping a stiff upper lip.

Family physicians report that possibly as high as 85 percent of their patients' illnesses have a psychosomatic component; I recently spoke to a divorce lawyer who told me one out of three of his clients has a matrimonial bad back (lower back pain). Fortunately, when we sense our feelings and change our feel/think/act, our psychosomatic illnesses and aches and pains will go away. Feeling bad and being sorry may have enabled us to survive when we were young, but they are not likely to bring us happiness in later life.

The Power of Positive Feelings

In 1976 I had a hunch that reliving early happy scenes would have the *same* therapeutic effect as reliving early traumatic scenes. The hunch proved false. However, I found that people were able to feel better and enjoy life more after a little practice in feeling happy. An interesting side effect was that clients who did happy regressions* rapidly developed the ability to go back and relive early traumatic scenes. It was as though they had built "memory muscles" and dissolved childhood amnesia.

As a matter of course, all clients who join my groups are

---

*Regressions here is the act of going back and reliving an earlier experience, which differs from the medical or psychoanalytic meaning, which usually involves a psychotic break or infantile behavior patterns.

taught to do happy regressions, and I have found that it is extremely important to do this with anyone who has been in psychoanalysis. Those who have been in psychoanalysis have been trained to free-associate (talk about) rather than reexperience, and to get strokes (recognition) for feeling bad; that is, their bad feelings are reinforced! At the end of this chapter, I will give a guided exercise so that you may go back and experience a happy early scene. It is important for some clients to experience, firsthand, that they have the power to give themselves happy feelings, although the average person seldom chooses to go back and think about a happy scene or relive a happy scene. What we do, because we are programmed that way, is to go back and relive the disasters.

In group sessions I ask the clients to pick a happy scene—from some five, ten, fifteen years ago, a really joyous experience, a peak experience they had—to keep it in mind, and then to let it go, and follow me as I take them through diaphragmatic breathing* and relaxation exercises. Then, when they're completely relaxed, I ask them to relive that early scene and to share it with the group if they wish to.

Many share with the group and tell how surprised they are at the difference in the quality of the memory when they relive rather than just talk about. After the client has been successful, guided fantasy is used to get back to an even earlier experience. The relaxed client is instructed:

"Pretend you are in a beautiful meadow on a warm day. You feel young, something nice happens, and you feel good or great. When you feel really good, look around you in the meadow, and you will see a sign with a number on it, stay with your good feelings, breathe deeply, don't think, tell me the number. (Client responds; if the client reports a number like forty-eight, the next intervention would be four or eight years old.) Breathe deeply, a scene will come to you when you were . . . years old and felt good. Relive the happy scene."

---

*In diaphragmatic breathing, the diaphragm is lowered when we inhale and raised when we exhale. It is the way we breathe when we are in a deep sleep, or the way we breathed as infants before we were frightened or tightened up by life experience. It is the *normal* way to breathe. As we breathe in, our stomach goes out, and as we breathe out, it comes in.

Many of us go through life raising our shoulders and sucking in our guts when we inhale; this is the opposite of normal breathing, and it takes a concerted effort to break this abnormal pattern. This abnormal type of shallow breathing helps us to block feelings and limits our oxygen intake. It is one of the ways we stop ourselves from living, since breath is life.

Further on in this chapter, both diaphragmatic breathing and relaxation exercises are illustrated.

Clinical Case

Elsie, aged thirty-eight, in group for fourteen weeks, had been hospitalized and had undergone shock treatment at thirty-six. She had no memories before she was thirteen, and "couldn't remember ever feeling good." She believed she was stupid, and would run a pattern of stupid, then scared, and then cry at each group session.

Fourteenth Session

Elsie: I have a recent scene, I'm with my girlfriends and we are out having a few drinks and talking. (Elsie looks happy, then her face changes to look sad and she begins to cry.) I wanted to go out with my husband, but he wouldn't take me.

Shep: Go back to feeling good with the girls. When did you have that feeling earlier?

Elsie: (Smiles, then begins to cry) I was on my honeymoon; I felt good, but then we only had a week and I had to go to work.

Fifteenth Session

Shep: Pretend you are in a meadow, and all the forest animals come out to play with you; you are safe. Something happens so that you feel great. (Pause) When you have that feeling, look around you, and you will see a sign with a number; tell me the number, don't think, stay with the good feeling, a scene will come to you.

Elsie: I'm eleven years old, I'm in New Hampshire running in the grass. It's great (looks sad), but then I got poison ivy . . .

Shep: Stay with the feeling and go back to an earlier scene.

Elsie: I'm ten years old, I'm in bed all alone; nobody can bother me here; I wake up and it's dark and I feel good.

Sixteenth Session

Elsie: I'm five years old; I'm at the beach; I'm playing in the waves . . . I feel great.

Eighteenth Session

Elsie: I'm two years old; my Grandma is playing with me . . . I feel good.

Four weeks later in group therapy, Elsie relived an early scene in which at age three she was teased and tortured by her five-year-old brother, and his friend, who kept jabbing her with sticks. She decided to be alone.

Six weeks later in group therapy, she relived a scene in which (as a two-year-old) she was having fun with her grandmother, wet her pants, and got beaten unmercifully. Later at the age of five, she relived getting caught in a wave and almost drowning at the beach. She decided it was very dangerous to feel good.

Five weeks later in group therapy, she reexperienced being raped at the age of ten by a seventeen-year-old uncle, who told her if she ever told anybody, he would kill her. She decided that it was better to be alone and (not remember) stay in the dark by playing stupid.

In thirty weeks of group therapy, Elsie made enormous changes, gave herself permission to be happy, and reported a tremendous improvement in her relationships with her friends, husband, and children.

The *power of positive feeling* cannot be underestimated. One client sat in group for ten weeks, a doubting Thomas, always sad, and never allowing herself to have good feelings. Each time I had the group do a "happy exercise," she would feel bad. One evening in group, while relaxed, she reported she smelled something baking, she got the scene, she was five years old at her grandma's house, and her grandma was baking bread. She relived the scene and had the feelings of being loved and happy. She subsequently made rapid and major changes in her life.

Experiment

I would like you to try out this experiment so that you can distinguish firsthand between reliving and talking about. I will give you instructions, and it may be helpful if you have a friend read them to you while you follow the instructions, or if you cut a tape recording of the instructions and play it to yourself.

You can be lying down or sitting down; for a beginning I suggest that you lie down on a very comfortable bed. Pick out a peak experience or a very happy experience—it can be five, ten, fifteen years ago. Think about it for a minute. Remember your feelings and your thoughts. And now, sitting or lying down (I will talk as though you were lying down), let yourself get very comfortable and let your body relax. Focus your awareness on your feet and on your toes, and let the tension drain out of your feet and toes. Now tighten up your toes as much as you can get them, and hold that position, and feel the tension and the stress of the muscle strain in your toes and in your feet. Now let go and let your feet relax.

Next tighten up the calves of your legs, get them real firm, feel the discomfort in the pulling of the muscle, hold for one breath and then let go. Now tighten up your thighs as firmly as you can get them, hold up for one long breath and then let go, let all the tension drain out of your lower limbs. Now tighten up your rear end as tight as you can get it, tighter, and now let go. Follow the above instructions for your stomach, shoulders, chest, neck, fists, lower forearms, biceps, eyes, ears, nose, mouth, jaw. And now focus your awareness on your breating, feel the breath as it enters and leaves your body; with each exhalation, let the tension drain out of your body. And now* imagine that your lungs are two balloons and that they are located in your tummy, around the waist. As you inhale, let those balloons come way up as they fill with air, so your stomach goes way out as you breathe in; then when those balloons are full of air, pull your stomach in, compress it, and push all the air out. Now wait; your body will breathe in by itslef. Finally tell your body to relax, and take five slow, deep breaths, letting the tension drain out of your body. Go back to that happy experience and relive it, be there, see the sights, smell the smells, hear the sounds, feel the feelings.

In my experience, people enjoy group therapy. Not everyone relives horrible early scenes; as a matter of fact, relatively few do, but even after reliving the most traumatic scenes, clients report that afterward they feel great. We do this work, and people make enormous changes in relatively short periods. The

---

*If you follow this part of the exercise, you will be doing diaphragmatic breathing. If you do not breathe this way normally, I suggest you practice five minutes every night at bedtime. By placing your hands on your abdomen, make sure your stomach comes up as you inhale. Do not be surprised if you feel peculiar or dizzy at first, especially if you are a smoker.

Incidentally, both men and women clients report that one side effect is that they have bigger orgasms.

average time in group therapy is perhaps twenty weeks, with some making the changes they desire in ten weeks, and others, those who have had shock treatment, have been institutionalized or hospitalized, or have had psychotic episodes, taking two to three years. Overall, I think we have seen remarkably rapid changes, with an extremely high percentage of the people accomplishing and achieving their goals within half a year, and then leading happier lives.

I attribute these results partly to the warm, secure, and loving environment and support of the group, partly to the happy regressions and guided fantasies, which are an enabling and empowering experience, and partially to deconditioning. If we can be conditioned to feel bad, we can decondition ourselves and feel good! There is a need to get in touch with our feelings.

Most of the time, therapy is fun and exciting. People enjoy changing.

If you were successful in the experiment, you should have had a vivid sensory experience with a high level of emotional feeling. Too many of us supress our capacities for joy, love, excitement, and happiness. What have we done to the child within us? Regardless of age, we are only as old we feel!

CHAPTER 11

The Karpman Triangle

Before continuing any discussion on feelings, I will define some terms: Persecutor, Rescuer, Victim, and Games.

Steve Karpman,* a San Francisco psychiatrist, has described the process of drama as changes in the psychological positions of three major basic roles: Persecutor, Victim, and Rescuer (see Figure 4). Drama is also heightened by changes in place (living room, dinging room, bedroom) in space (private/public) and in location (Meanwhile, back on the ranch, Ma and Pa Kettle . . .), and the velocity of the changes.

For instance, in the drama of Little Red Riding Hood, Little Red Riding Hood's mom sends her through the woods to take lunch to Grandma. Mom is Rescuer to Grandma, Persecuter to Little Red. What kind of mother sends her daughter into the woods without warning her about talking wolves. Grandma is sick, lives alone in the woods, and leaves her door unlocked! On the way, Little Red Riding Hood meets a talking wolf, to whom she tells all about Grandma being alone in the house. Little Red, playing Victim, sets up the wolf to Persecute Grandma. Then she naively stays and dawdles in the forest to pick flowers. The wolf hotfoots it over to Grandma's house and eats her. When

*Steven Karpmen, "Fairy Tales and Script Drama Analysis," *Transactional Analysis Bulletin,* April 1968.

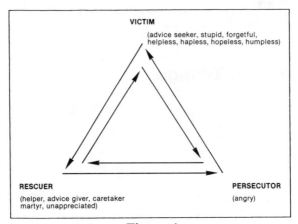

Figure 4
Karpman's Triangle: Drama is provided
by a switch in roles.

Little Red Riding Hood arrives, the wolf, disguised as Grandma, tries to talk her into getting in bed with him. "Grandma, what big eyes you have . . . what big teeth you have," says Little Red Riding Hood, still naive, even stupid. However, she finally figures out what's going on and runs out in the nick of time and finds a woodcutter, a Rescuer, who kills the wolf, cuts its stomach open, and rescues Grandma. The wolf is now the Victim.

A mother who'd pull a stunt like Mrs. Red Riding Hood would wind up either a martyr, sad at the loss of her daughter; or if Little Red Riding Hood returns, Mom would be stuck again with an instigator.

Grandma* is interesting. She lives in the woods with the door unlocked, probably waiting for a talking wolf to come and eat her. The wolf probably supplied the greatest excitement in her life in the last ten or fifteen years, and Grandma must have been pretty frustrated when she got "rescued."

If Grandma was capable of living in the woods alone, she was certainly capable of getting her own lunch. Grandma, in-

*The story of Little Red Riding Hood was written in the days when people got married and had children when young. Since Little Red is just a kid, Grandma may well be in her late thirties or early forties.

cidentally, had a miraculous recovery after the woodcutter got her out of the wolf's stomach. Evidently being eaten was very agreeable to Grandma. At this point I might add that the child part of us does not age. Grandmas can be just as much fun-loving, sexy kids as any teenagers, if not more so!

In real life, Rescuers doing what the woodcutter did are often sued and prosecuted! The Rescuer would probably serve fourteen years for second-degree wolf-slaughter. If this didn't happen, when he got home you can imagine the dialogue between the woodcutter and his wife when she asked, "Well, where's the wood?" When he answered that he had spent the day rescuing Grandma and Little Red Riding Hood, you can hear her say, if she believed him, "Hey, you're always doing for other people, but if I ask you to do anything around the house you're not here . . ." If she didn't believe him, more likely this could lead to a first-class game.

To the degree that you're involved in the drama triangle in real life, you are suffering and feeling bad no matter what your favorite life role is. The Persecutor is a Victim on a psychological level. He or she really wants love and positive recognition and is doing what he or she *thinks* is best for the other person (not what *is* best), feeling unappreciated and earning hatred and negative recognition.

Several years ago I had to be in Marion, Illinois, at 9:00 A.M. and flew a major airline into St. Louis the night before. The airline had made a reservation for me on an 8:20 P.M. connecting flight from St. Louis to Carbondale (Marion is eighteen miles from there), and the estimated time of arrival in Carbondale, Illinois, was 9:00 P.M. I figured I would get a good night's sleep and drive to Marion in the morning.

When I arrived in St. Louis at 7:30 P.M., I carried my 30.5-pound luggage four blocks to the Air Illinois terminal for the connecting flight. Air Illinois told me that the major airline's computer had made a mistake and there was no 8:20 P.M. flight. The next flight wasn't until 6:00 A.M.

With smoke shooting out of my ears, I dragged myself and my luggage back to the airline office. By this time, the decimal had dropped out of the 30.5 pounds and I was ugly! I chewed out the innocent ticket agent, "What do you SOB's mean

by . . .'' "But, Dr. Gellert, we will put you up in a motel.''
"Shove it . . .'' To the observer, I must have looked like a
homicidal maniac, a Persecutor. Believe me, I felt very much a
victim.

Rescuers are also Victims. While Rescuers are taking care of
everybody else's needs, they are persecuting themselves by not
taking care of their own needs. Furthermore, Rescuers are doing
for other people what they are fully capable of doing for
themselves, keeping the helpless helpless. Rescuers play martyr
and resent it, or get depressed when they are not rescuing,
because no one needs them at that time. Rescuers also feel
unloved and unappreciated, are doing what they *think* is best
for the other person (not what *is* best), and are earning resentment and negative recognition.

I listened to the Lone Ranger for about eight years and never
once did he fall in love with a pretty girl or have fun. Come to
think of it, neither did Tom Mix or Hopalong Cassidy. The
Lone Ranger spent his life being a good guy, helping everybody,
and what was his payoff? In the end, they took away his mask.

Signs of the changing times and our moral values in Western
culture are the current Westerns, James Bond films, and space
odyssies. The heroes always get women, over and over again,
which means that they never have any close relationships. Plen-
ty of sex, but no love, warmth, or intimacy.

Both Persecutor and Rescuer roles are top dog, bossy, one
up, parental roles; that is, both Persecutor and Rescuer act as
parents. The victim role is the not-okay child role, the victim
acts as a not-okay child! Age has nothing to do with the roles we
play.

Descriptive adjectives, although oversimplifications, readily
identify the various roles people play when they are in any of
these slots in real life. The Victim can play Scared, Kick Me,
Stupid, Loser of Things, Klutz, Schlemiel, Procrastinator,
Forgetful. In general, the Victim is a charter member of the 4-H
club: Helpless, Hapless, Hopeless, and Humpless. When in-
teracting with others, the Victim tries to get the Persecutor to
kick him or her. When the Victim gets the Persecutor to kick,
the world sees that the Persecutor is not okay. When the Victim
gets the Rescuer to rescue him or her, he or she then defeats the
Rescuer by not being rescued at all or by not staying

rescued—by getting into the next jam, or by escalating disasters. He or she shows the Rescuer that no matter what is done, it's not enough, and the Rescuer is wrong!

The Rescuer position can be described as helper, adviser, caretaker, and the like. The heaviest Rescuer is the smothering father or mother who programs his or her children to be schizophrenic. Recently, in giving a course to mental health workers for New York State, one of the social workers reported he had a schizophrenic client whose mother wiped his rear end up to the age of fourteen!

The Persecutor usually needs no adjectives, since his or her anger/criticality describe him or her as not okay.

In his original article, Steve Karpman mentions the audience in dramas, but the audience really turns the triangle into a pyramid with a fourth role in real life, that of Voyeur. The Voyeur, Onlooker, Instigator, or Peeping Tom can enter the drama at any point as the Persecutor, Rescuer, or Victim. My co-therapist, Grace Wilson, and I once had a male Little Red Riding Hood in group who was superb at setting up "let's you-and-she fight" situations. Five minutes after the client entered the room, Grace and I would be in an argument. On a psychological level, a Voyeur is also a Victim. He or she is not living, is not fully alive, if he or she gets life's thrills or chills from watching other people fight or from watching "Kojak" or "Deep Throat." Voyeurs are not living when vicariously satisfying their needs for sex, excitement, or mayhem. The idea of the Voyeur is a useful concept in understanding family systems, because very often family games are played out for the satisfaction of the Voyeur or the Instigator. How many of us have secretly gloated while watching our siblings catch it or our spouse fighting with, or being put down by, one of our children.

Games

When people act like Persecutor-Rescuer-Victim in their relationships, they wind up with bad feelings. A unit of such interaction is called a game. Nobody wins a game, but the prize each player gets is bad feelings. Logically, once we know we are going to feel bad, we should avoid games. However, without awareness, we are illogical in personal relationships.

Many of us are programmed to be bad-feeling "junkies";

we need our daily "fix." Furthermore, if no one is around to play with, we play solitaire: Persecute (kick) ourselves or play Victim (martyr, unappreciated, etc.), by leaving the here and now and reviewing a past, or fantasizing a future, disaster. It's like masturbating, but we can keep it up longer.

Karpman's Triangle is magnificent in its simplicity, with practical applications in psychotherapy and self-therapy. Games—i.e., repetitive series of transactions between people, resulting in bad feelings—can be analyzed in detail using the roles and process Karpman described.

In the following chapters, I will be using these terms to describe couples and family interactions, but first to return to feelings.

CHAPTER 12

What Is This Thing Called Love?

Happy Couples Relationship

Little kids love to play with each other. Take a couple of kids to the beach or on a picnic, and right away they look for other kids to play with. They don't want to know the other kids' social status, school grades, racial background, religion, neighborhood. They just want to play and have fun.

A good couples relationship has a lot of Child-to-Child interactions. Instead of each person *taking care of the other person,* he or she is taking care of himself or herself, and in the process each has desires for joy, fun, and love fulfilled. When little kids are playing together, they are not looking to please each other; they are looking to please themselves and in the process they will please each other. A happy couple do together things they both enjoy. They have a social life, friends, some common interests, and an *interest in each other.* The attitude of the Persecuting or Rescuing parent toward a Child is not present, because both are grown-ups. They nurture and are nurtured, which is far different from being rescued. All of us, regardless of age, at one time or another need nurturing: tender loving care. In a good relationship, if one person is sick or down or breaks a leg, the other one will provide support, compassion, and tender loving care (TLC) *if the one who is down wants it!* This situation is different from the Rescuer situation. In the latter the other person must be down to be okay, so the rescuer breaks the other person's legs so he can support that person. Real rescuers are fire fighters and lifeguards, not Caretakers, Advice Givers, and Helpers.

The happy couple are together because they *want* to be with each other, not because they *need* to be with each other! They also have outside sources of stroking (recognition), such as friends, interest in music, bridge, baseball, art, business, a hobby or *internal* resources, yoga, meditation, religion, so they are not dependent on each other as sole sources of strokes. They accept each other, and if one is down, the other allows that one the space to withdraw, feel bad, get angry or experience some other feeling. The one is not wanting the other to change. Sex is not a problem; it is a pleasure!

Unhappy Couples Relationship

For the infant to survive, it is necessary that Mom and Dad do for the child things that he* is not capable of doing for himself, like tying the three-year-old's shoe. If the parents are still tying the child's shoes when he's eleven years old, or taking care of him when he's thirty-five, then we have the unhealthy situation in which the child is trained to be dependent (Victim) and the parents are in the Rescuing or smothering role, keeping the Victim helpless. He has been programmed not to use his computer (to problem-solve, to be responsible or considerate) when in the presence of his parents.

Mom and Dad can't meet his sex needs when he grows up, so he will find a woman like his mother or his father and attempt to set her up in the same situation he had with this parents. If he is strong enough, his wife will be in the Parent role (Persecutor or Rescuer), and he will be in the Child role (Victim). He'll be passive and want a good nurturing mommy to take care of him. He, however, will not take care of her needs/wants to be nurtured, loved, have fun, or her need for recognition. It is not the job of little kids to love parents; it is the job of parents to love

---

*In all examples, "he" or "she" is interchangeable.

little kids. Little kids want to play. They come into the house and they want Mommy or Daddy to comfort them and to hug them when they want to be hugged. He (the Victim) will just want her (Persecutor-Rescuer) present, but he will not want to play with her, hug her, recognize her.

We've all witnessed a department store scene in which a mother is holding her child by the hand with an iron grip, and the kid is struggling to get away. That child's idea of happiness is to be left alone. Then there's the other kind of mother, who ignores her child completely, and the little kid is hanging onto Mommy's dress for dear life, afraid of abandonment. Later in life these two kids meet, and as long as they relate Child to Child, it's great. But after coupling, when the "novocaine" wears off, one of them has the idea that to be left alone is heaven, and the other one's idea of heaven is to be held. Soon the man (assuming he withdraws from his wife) will discover that he is coupled to an angry, hostile, and resentful parent figure. If she isn't angry and hostile when she marries him, she'll become that way in no time at all. Sooner or later, in this situation, she may look elsewhere to get her wants met: have an affair, live through the children, get a job, go to graduate school, join the bridge club, or the Red Cross—anything to fill time while waiting for him to grow up!

The couple stay with each other because they *need* each other, not because they *want* each other. What they *want* is for the other to change. There is a great difference between need and want. I *need* air, water, food, and shelter. Without them, I will die! I do not *need* love; without it, I will just be unhappy, and most of us live out our lives being unhappy, to some degree. If I need my spouse, I am saying that without her I will die. As an infant I needed Mommy, or I would have died! If I *need* to be with you, then on some level I will resent you. If I *want* to be with you, I am free to enjoy you and you will *feel wanted*. Think about it. This is not just semantics! To feel loved, you must feel wanted. The following case will illustrate some typical long-term unhappy relationships.

Alcoholic and Spouse

If the husband has the drinking problem, he is in the Child

slot, and his wife is set up to be his Persecuting/Rescuing parent. In society, she usually plays the heavy game of martyr. She's usually proper, a hard worker; she doesn't use abusive language, tell off-color stories, and may even be a "goody-two-shoes." She's neat and has a bad back (early childhood anger) or a bad neck. She's usually the salt of the earth, a good church-going lady, and a compulsive house cleaner.

He plays 'helpless' with his drinking problem and is delightful to the world when sober. He usually cannot express anger at women (wife, mother); when sober, he will say, "My wife is a fine woman. I don't know how she puts up with me." From the Victim (Child) slot, he actively persecutes the family by smashing the car, spending the paycheck, coming home drunk, and throwing up on the rug. "It's not my fault—it's the demon rum."

When he gets off the sauce, there may be a role reversal, and he will become a Critical Parent (Persecutor) and expect the family to kiss his backside in Macy's window because today he didn't get drunk. He spends most of his time in the Parent role, extremely righteous, and it's not uncommon to hear his wife say, "I was better off when he was drinking."

If the wife is the problem drinker, the man is usually neat, prissy, prim, "goody-two-shoes," a compulsive house cleaner, with a bad back or neck pains—the exact same profile as the female spouse of a drinker.

It is easy to diagnose this system. If I am talking to a woman or a man for about five minutes and I feel that I need a drink, I usually ask, "Does your spouse have a drinking problem?"

The Workaholic Couple

The workaholic comes in type A and type B, depending on the strength of the spouses. The *stronger* one always wins the Victim slot.* To illustrate the workaholic, I will use the average doctor, although the same picture is seen in rich men, poor men, beggars, thieves, lawyers, and Indian chiefs.

Type A: On the job, the physician is a Rescuer to his patients and a Persecutor to the nurses. But when he gets home, he may

---

*Contrary to popular belief, anyone who thinks they are "strong" and coupled to a "weak" spouse, can tell you how ineffective they are at producing change!

well take the Victim role, with his wife playing Persecutor. She will be angry, hostile, and critical, because she is not getting her wants met, namely, her wants for companionship, to be taken care of, appreciated, respected, loved. How can she, when he's working anywhere from ten to fourteen hours a day? Consciously or unconsciously, blatantly or subtly, she will give the children the message that the father is not okay and they will reinforce it!

Type B: If the wife is stronger than the husband, she will preempt the child slot. He will be a Persecutor to her, outraged because not only does he have to carry the burden of the world on his shoulders in his medical practice, but when he comes home he is still stuck in the role of caretaker. If she is strong, she's probably strong enough to set the children up to take care of her and abandon the parenting role. This now leaves the overloaded doctor with the task of taking care of the children. She can easily have him do this by being accident prone, or better yet by having a nervous breakdown (going crazy)—then she can persecute everybody. Since drugs are available, she can become a "drugaholic," "a sickaholic," or and alcoholic. The children don't get much of Dad's attention, so one of the ways they can get him to notice them is by getting sick, being thrown out of school, being picked up by the police, or engaging in other self-destructive behavior. They can need his time and money for getting out of trouble, for help, aid, and assistance when they are ten, twenty, and fifty years old.

If the doctor is making $200,000 a year, the family system will manage to spend $200,010 a year. As a group, doctors are much respected, much maligned, and much persecuted. The doctors and spouses I see for couples' counseling are usually on their second marriage. They had been married to a type A, swore they wouldn't make the same mistake, and chose a type B, or vice versa.

My choice of the medical profession for the illustration of the workaholic was not accident. Here is a fine example of a little kid trained not to take care of his or her own wants and needs. The programming usually excludes joy and happiness. Instead, the doctor is trained to be a Rescuer and to take care of other people. In the process, he or she persecutes himself or herself and the entire family. Who takes care of the caretaker?*

Spouse Beater

Usually (not always) in a couples system, where the man is physically abusing the woman, it is very difficult to get the woman to go to family court to stop him from beating her, or to get her to leave him, regardless of financial circumstances!

Usually the wife is in the Parent slot, playing martyr. The husband looks a little "weird"† and is in the victim slot. She zaps him constantly; no matter what he says, he's not right. She constantly criticizes him, but not overtly; she does it in a very fine and polite manner. For example, if he says, "It's a beautiful day," she'll say, "You know, Henry, last year it was twelve degrees warmer."

He'll ask for another helping of sausages and she'll say, "You know they're not good for you, Henry." Usually she will not appear angry or hostile; rather, she's an underground fighter, either rescuing or persecuting: "I'm only trying to help you, Henry," or "I could never hate you" (meaning there's something wrong with me, because you're extremely despicable). Finally, after she gives him enough of these subtle darts, he blows his stack and gives her twenty stitches. The exception to the above description is when the man is psychotic or paranoid schizophrenic, and then he will fantasize put-downs in order to give her twenty stitches.

In working with women such as the one described above, I find that they usually had one parent who physically abused them when they were young. To them, love is being physically abused. The Rescuers of the world always turn white with anger when they hear me say this. They say, "How can you talk this way about the poor victim?" What they cannot see is that the victim is also a persecutor. This is not to condone abuse; I work immediately to stop any violence, potential and actual. There is emotional abuse, which is just as bad as physical abuse. Abuse is abuse, whether it is verbal or physical.

---

*In my experience, as a class, mental health professionals have far worse couples relationships than physicians.

†It is impossible to describe the weird look; you have to see one. Every wife beater, flasher, child molester I've had in therapy has had a similar look. The best description I can give is that these people look very young in chronological age, and their eyes have a strange, glassy look.

In unhappy relationships, there is an interlocking and mutual Rescue-Persecution going on. Each partner rescues the other, at the same time persecuting each other, and each feels that he or she is the Victim.

I am amazed at how stable really bad marriages are. I attribute the stability to two factors, which are actually two facets of the same thing: (1) fighting old wars and (2) fear of abandonment.

Fighting Old Wars

In 1975, I read in the newspaper that a Japanese soldier had surrendered on one of the Pacific Islands. He had been fighting World War II for thirty years, after everyone else had quit. If you think this is amusing, it isn't. Most of us spend our lives fighting old wars long after the war has ended. How many of us are still looking to get our parents' approval, and if by chance we do get it, it doesn't count, because we are not four or five years old. Very often we recreate the old battles, outside of our awareness, hoping that this time we will win. It never happens; again we are not four or five years old, and our spouse is not our parent. We try to resolve these ancient wars by marrying Mom who wouldn't love us, or Dad who always put us down, or an uncle who molested us.

A client I was seeing in individual therapy told me that the preceeding week she had found me very seductive and was angry at me. I thought back to that week: I had been sad and had been thinking about problems. Believe me, when I'm being seductive I know it. I asked her if sad men with problems excited her. She had already mentioned that between the ages of seven and eleven, she had been sexually used by her father, who, throughout her childhood, had problems and felt sad. This experience led her to the awareness that sad men with problems turned her on. When she found a sad man with problems, she could then start the war, not play. When she met a happy man or a man without problems, she felt no attraction toward him. She was in therapy because her relationship with men had been one disaster after another. She made and kept the contract (agreement) that when she met a sad man with problems, she would run, and when she met a happy man without problems, she would date him. She followed this resolution but found out that she was scared of happy men and felt comfortable only when "helping" sad men solve their problems. It took a while for her to work through her fear of success and happiness, but eventually she overcame it.

This brings us to the question, "What is this thing called love?" Certainly, the term "love" has many meanings, one of them being fear of abandonment.

• A client described her relationship with her boyfriend. He criticized her, insulted her, called her names, compared her unfavorably to previous girlfriends, made promises and dates he didn't keep; and their sex life was lousy. He had other undesirable traits. I asked, "Why do you stay with him?" She said, "Because I love him." What's to love? This is not love, this is fear of abandonment.

• A twenty-three-year-old client had a forty-year-old boyfriend who was married and had three children. She was working and he sponged from her. He would see her only on weekends, when he could give his wife the excuse that he was going out of town to work. He was hostile, critical, put his girlfriend down, stood her up, told her she was lousy in bed; when I asked her why she stayed with him, she said, "Because I love him." This wasn't love; he was her father, and this was fear of abandonment. If she took enough abuse and worked hard enough, father would not leave.

Ruth and Les

Ruth and Les, both therapists, had recently split up. Ruth was extremely rational, nonfeeling, cold, critical, unlovable, withdrawn, and strong. She had been the parent figure. Les was extremely childlike, warm, creative, intuitive, loving, accepting. Ruth, his soul mate, had left him. In most relationships, usually the aggressive one in the relationship is the passive one in bed and vice versa. This was an exception. Ruth was the aggressive one in the relationship and in bed. After they split-up, Les had other women, but complained that nobody was as good as Ruth in bed. I sympathized with him on this point, until I found out that in bed he would lie there passively while she performed fellatio. He was the young infant and she was the mommy, and this was their main modus operandi in the sex area.

I see nothing wrong with oral sex, as long as it is turn taking or mutual. However, in any relationship that is a one-way street, something disastrous is going on. Ruth was reinforcing his infantile needs, and she was not having orgasms. She was in the giving role and was the Rescuer in bed and the Critical Parent everywhere else. Les was obsessing, all he could think of was Ruth, and almost had a nervous breakdown. It took all our efforts to keep him from being hospitalized. He finally was successful in working through and giving up this "precious gem." In a way, he had the best of both worlds: in bed Ruth was his mother who had kept him helpless and dependent, a big baby, and in a day-to-day relationship she was his father who was hostile, angry, and critical. No wonder the attraction was so strong!

Ruth was this tower of strength only in relation to Les or when she was in the parent role. With therapists she supervised or people "one down," she was a terror. When in the presence of authority figures or people "one up," she was sweetness and light, compliant. If anyone confronted her with her hyper-criticality and her need to criticize people and put them down, she would go all to pieces, become hysterical, and run to her supervisor or get other people to rescue her. Who could blame her for her behaviour, when she had had such a bad early childhood? (Her mother had been a prostitute during World War II and had gone from army base to army base in a trailer, taking little Ruth with her.)

All through their relationship, Ruth had constantly put Les down and, intellectually, Les was fully in touch with all her shortcomings, and was aware of how lousy the relationship outside of bed had been. But when asked why Les kept hanging on to Ruth, he would say, with his voice quivering and body shaking, "I love her."

Love is a word that has been used universally and has never been satisfactorily defined in the field of psychology. There is a feeling of love, a feeling of warmth, of well-being, of serenity, and when combined with sex, it's great. Great isn't the right word, it's a ne-plus-ultra (there is no better) feeling. If I love you, I accept you as you are. I'm not looking to change you. Unfortunately, most of the romantic novels and Hollywood emphasize the infantile euphoria of finding Mom or Dad. The flip side of infantile euphoria *is* the fear of abandonment, a sinking feeling in the guts, accompanied by despair.

Some of us spend little time in euphoria and much in despair—the black hole, nothingness—hoping to find Mr or Ms Right so we can experience infantile euphoria. I myself spent forty-six years in the black hole, with possibly eight or ten hours of euphoria. Being grown up means giving up the euphoria and the despair and living with the disappointment that we will never win the war, find the ideal (Mom or Dad), prince or princess charming, without making ourselves sad or angry because we were cheated. Rather than alternate from infantile euphoria to black despair, happiness involves staying in the mid-range, in the here and now, accepting what is and doing for ourselves things that make us happy. This is tough when so many of us know that in order to be happy all we have to do is to get our spouse to change. Of course, they haven't in our last 9,999 tries, but maybe next time they will hear us!

Fear of Abandonment

As I have described earlier, infants need physical touching to survive. When they are not getting recognition, either positive or negative, they may *feel* abandoned. The feeling is indescribable—a wrenching, twisting, sickness in the guts, wanting to throw up, despair and misery and fear. To avoid the feelings of abandonment, I believe we go through life accepting and even conjuring negative stroking and other bad feelings, being put down, staying married to alcoholics, schizophrenics, child abusers, wife beaters, child molesters, and worse. Some clients eventually recall scenes in which their parents told them they were going to give them away, throw them out, lock them out of the house. Some even took their children for a walk in the woods and lost them for an hour or two because they misbehaved. As grown-ups these clients did not remember their unpleasant experiences; they just wondered why they were so scared of people (their parents) and why they stayed in miserable marriages.

Fear of abandonment holds people together in unpleasant,

unhappy marriages. The bad feelings generated by the relationship (fear, anger, depression, impulses toward suicide,
homicide) are better than the dreaded fear of being alone, of being abandoned.

Ted

Ted, a thirty-six-year-old man, wanted to get a divorce. But
every time he moved out of the house, he became panicky and
moved back and promptly became depressed. We knew from
previous work that when Ted was two years old, his parents
discovered that his older brother, aged five, was retarded, and
promptly sent the brother away. They never visited or talked
about this brother. Although Ted was aware that his brother
had been sent away, he had never tied it into his own particular
predicament. His goal in coming into group therapy was to be
stong enough to be able to leave his unhappy marriage. Incidentally, Ted was extremely wealthy and could not use the money
problem as an excuse for not getting a divorce.

Shep: Relax and stay with the feeling. When did you have
this feeling of panic when you were little? Let a scene
come to you. (Ted is in regression.)

Ted: I was three or four. I was walking with my parents,
and I would run ahead of them and hide, then they
would find me. I ran and hid, but they didn't come,
so I came out and looked for them. I couldn't see
them. I had the same feeling of panic. They were
hiding, watching me.

Shep: What did you decide?

Ted: To keep an eye on them so they wouldn't lose me.

Shep: (Key intervention) You knew they might not be playing. You had previous information they might want
to lose you. Something had happened earlier. What
was it?

Ted: (Sits for several minutes thinking, then starts to shake
all over.) I was two years old, I got lost in a department store. My mother told me I was bad. I was
afraid they would send me away like my brother
because they didn't like me.

Shep: So what did you decide?

Ted: I decided not to trust them, to do what they wanted
            me to do, to be resentful, not to let them know how I
            felt, and to wait till I grew up.

Ted subsequently decided not to wait any longer; he came to
the decision to end his unhappy marriage without feeling panic
and abandonment, rather than stay and feel resentful and
depressed.

I cannot stress enough how powerful and terrifying the fear
of being abandoned is. The power of fear of abandonment in
shaping, bending, or breaking the young child is awesome. I had
a client who was having "problems" with her six-year-old son.
He had school phobia and would vomit when she left him at
school, and when she picked him up he would cling to her. He
wouldn't leave the house to play down the street; he would
always hand around.

I asked her how long this behavior had been going on. She
said that he had never been this way when younger. He used to
love going to prenursery school and day school, but one day he
had "changed overnight" when he was around three-and-a-half
years old. I asked her, "What happened the day before the
morning you took him to school and he was changed?" She told
me she had driven the station wagon to do some shopping; the
child was with her. Because he had fallen asleep on the way
home, she left him asleep in the car while she unloaded the station wagon, carried the packages to the kitchen, and put away
her groceries. She says he couldn't have been in the car more
than ten minutes. As soon as she unpacked, she went out to
wake him up and found him awake, screaming and crying.
Many children have similar traumas or get lost in department
stores or at picnics but don't develop phobias. One scene can
have this effect, however, if the child feels that he is unwanted.
In this case, the father was "never home" (successful
businessman) for the child, and the mother was very active
socially (seldom home).

I'm Bad

Little kids cannot run away from home, so in order to survive many clients protect their parents by thinking that they
themselves are bad. Their need to see their parents as being nor-

mal clouds their vision. An extreme example of this is a client who had multiple personalities. She reported a scene in which when she was three-and-a-half years old, she was in the garden pulling leaves off the cabbages. Her mother punished her by dragging her into the house and putting her hands on a red-hot skillet on the stove. She said, "My mother had to do that to stop me from picking cabbage leaves. I was bad." I asked her if she had told her father about the incident. She said, "No, he would have killed her if I did." When we examine the client's statements, we notice that they are not logical. It does occur to the client (a) that her mother had options other than burning her hands, (b) that if her father had known about the incident and would therefore have killed her mother, he evidently wouldn't have thought her mother had done a good thing, (c) that pulling leaves off cabbages was probably fun for a three-year-old. She had married a man who was a wife beater. It was only after reliving the scene that she could leave him.

Another extreme example was Nola, who relived a scene in which her father was drunk and tried to strangle her when she was three years old. She screamed, and her mother and grandmother ran into the room. At knife-point they locked him out of the house and never let him back in. The incident precipitated a divorce.

Nola said, "I should have let him kill me. I ruined my parent's marriage." After some work, she realized that if her father had killed her, he would have been put in an insane asylum and her parents wouldn't have lived happily ever after. If this sounds crazy, it is!

Nola had been in an extremely destructive relationship with a married man and was only able to leave him after she had done this particular piece of work and had understood that if she stood up for herself, she would not ruin her mother's life!

When I was forty-eight years old, I myself worked through my own fear of abandonment. When I was three-and-a-half years old, my father took me to a large market about ten blocks from our house, where fruit, vegetables, pickles, groceries, cheese, and other products were being sold. When we left the food market, my father took me to a toy store two doors past the market. After looking at the toys, I turned around and found that my father was gone. I knew instantly that I had been abandoned because he didn't like me. I thought of walking back to the market, going from stall to stall, and asking if anyone wanted to adopt a little boy. I knew nobody would like a little boy who cries, so I didn't cry. But when I left the toy store, I looked around and saw my father standing behind a telephone pole, about twenty feel away, watching me with a *peculiar smile* on his face. In retrospect, I know he was training me not to feel scared. Somehow this kind of parental training in insecurity never works to make kids feel fearless and safe; it has the opposite effect!

This experience had been in my memory and I had often talked about it but had never unlocked it until, as part of my training as a therapist, I was at a confrontive therapy workshop. It was during the workshop that I relived this scene. It came to me as I was standing in a corner! I saw the windows of the toy store, became terrified, and cried like a baby. It was so overwhelming that I would have fallen if two people hadn't held me up. During that early scene—when I was three-and-a-half, when I had walked out of the store and seen my father—I knew I had not been abandoned, but the decision not to feel scared, not to let anyone know how scared I was, and not to cry was extremely powerful and on a gut level, and still a part of me. At three-and-a-half I thought that my father took me back because I didn't cry! I thought if I had cried or acted scared, he would have left me, and he was smiling because I was a "good boy." Later in life I married my father and stayed in a disastrous marriage for many, many years because of my fear of abandonment.

One Parent Wasn't There

In the couples in which one is the parent and the other is the child, it's obvious that the one who is playing Big Mommy or Big Daddy is taking care of the other one's fear of abandonment. What is not obvious, and is difficult to explain and to grasp, is that the one who is in the child slot is also a parent figure, taking care of the other one's fear of abandonment. For example, a woman cast in the slot of Mommy is taking care of hubby, who is the big baby. When the woman was growing up, one of her parents was not, in truth, a full parent. It could have been either her mother or her father, but one of them was more a child in the family system than a parent and was not there for her. The husband, the big baby, is for his wife either her mother or her father. So, psychologically, the husband is one of the woman's parents, and she can fight the old war to get hubby-child (Mom or Dad) to take care of her, and can lose again!

As I said, this isn't easy to grasp. Here's a personal example: My father was both a critical parent and a nurturing parent to me. My mother was a child to him in their relationship and just wasn't there for me as a critical or nurturing parent. Her attitude toward her children was that we were things, or that my sister was her rival for my father's affection and attention. So my mother performed certain parental functions. The women I've picked have been either my father or my mother. If they were my mother, then I became the Persecutor/Rescuer parent. When I picked my father, I became the depressed, withdrawn child, the unhappy, sad child Victim. Like my mother, I performed certain parental functions, such as earning a living; taking care of the bills, the cars, the plumbing in the house; chauffeuring kids, but I was not there for my wife as a warm, loving human being, and not there for my children as a loving parent.

"The Rich Get Richer and the Poor Get Poorer"

If both our parents are warm, loving, touching, give us positive strokes when we are growing up, and are there for us when we need them, then we will not have fear of abandonment to drive us into relationships to fight old wars (or at least not this old war). If our parents are warm, loving, touching, and give positive strokes to each other, then when we grow up we will pick a spouse who is warm, loving, touching, and gives positive strokes. If our parents' marriage is a disaster, we will recreate the disaster.

CHAPTER 13

Nuts Come In Pairs

Those of us who are programmed to feel bad, i.e., bad-feeling junkies, will couple up, unfortunately, on the basis of our programmed bad feelings, so that we can get our fix. In my experience, in almost every instance, nuts come in pairs. The holes in his head match the rocks in hers, and vice versa.

We select our spouse on the basis of many subliminal cues, well below the level of awareness—pupil size, pupil dilation, body gestalt, minute facial expressions, secret nonverbal messages, possibly even chemically—but select we do, and almost invariably the guy with macho meets the girl with machette, and vice versa.

We get our bad-feelings fix by playing *games*: repetitive series of transactions that result in our having our favorite bad feeling.

Before marriage or coupling, even a casual boy-girl relationship will reflect the game possibilities. I will illustrate with one of the many possibilities: Teaser.

Miss Low Self-Esteem (L.S.E.) meets Mr. Nice Guy (N.G.), who also has low self-esteem. Nice guys are in the business of pleasing everybody and they're usually depressed. N.G. sees L.S.E. and he says, "Hubba, hubba." He has woman on a pedestal because he had his mother on a pedestal. What he *wants* is a girl who will do everything, any time, any where. So he dates her five or ten times, thinking, "If I'm nice to her, maybe she'll give me sex." Meanwhile, she's thinking, "Ah, he appreciates and respects the real me." *So the man gives love, hoping to get sex.** On the eleventh date, he makes a pass at her and she says, "Oh, you're a beast. You're after that one thing all beasts want."

He now walks away feeling rejected, sad, put down, thinking, "Women will do it to you every time." He knows this because his "Mama done told" him when he was in knee pants. She goes away feeling lonely and resentful, thinking, "I'll never find Mr. Right."

This is not to imply that Miss Low Self-Esteem is a virgin. When she meets a real beast it's love at first sight and she will go to bed with him. The beast believes women are sluts because his mother was a slut, so he will dump her after a one night stand, since he is looking for "Virginia Good Girl." Eventually she will find and marry a beast who will constantly criticize her and put her down, or she'll find and marry a nice guy whom she can criticize and put down.

Couples' Games

What's for Supper?

After marriage and after the honeymoon is over (the anesthetic wears off), the couple will settle down to lifetime gaming. Mr. Beast comes home with a need to be angry and criticize his wife, so he walks into the kitchen and growls, "What's for supper?" and she says, "Pheasant under glass." He says, "Ugh, I had it for lunch." I had a couple who played this major game often. She was a beautiful, twenty-six-year-old, a creative, talented commercial artist, and he was a salesman whose main interest in life was baseball and beer. He'd come home and go through the house looking for something to nag her about. I asked her to prepare a list of twenty-six things that were wrong in the house, and to hand it to him when he walked

*Usually. As our society is changing, role reversal is occurring more and more!

in the door and say, "No need to go through the house and get angry, just pick whichever one you want to criticize me for." Of course the game broke up; so did the marriage. He split when she would no longer take his insults and put-downs. She persecuted him from the Victim slot by withdrawing, withholding sex, and letting him subtly know that she was far more cultured, educated, and intelligent than he (which she was). She *was willing to change*, but he was not. She went back to work and today is a very successful commercial artist.

In the preceding game, he was in the Persecutor role. Games are also played in which one of the married couple is in the rescuer role, that is to say, persecutes from the Rescue position.

What's the Matter, Dear?*

She: What's the matter, dear?

He: Nothing's the matter, darling.

She: Well, there must be something the matter or you wouldn't be sitting there acting that way.

He: No, nothing's the matter. I'm just thinking about the office.

She: Well, if nothing's the matter, how come you haven't mowed the lawn or done any of the things around the house that need doing? How come you're just sitting there?

He: Well, if you have to know what's the matter, it's you. You're always nagging, "What's the matter?"

When I read the above dialogue to my group once, one of the women put her hands to her face and said, "My God, that's me. I've been doing that with my husband for twenty-eight years, seven times a week."

Like this couple, couples lean on each other, with one of them taking the position, "I'm okay," and the other one, "I'm not okay." The one who's okay is trying to change the other one. If the not-okay spouse ever straightens up, the other one has either to straighten up also or to fall down.

---

*Described by Ray Poindexter, a Northridge, California, psychiatrist, in a brilliant theoretical article, "The Excluded Parent and Child in Game Theory," *Transactional Analysis Journal*, July 1972.

In the "What's the matter, dear?" system, when he is not okay, she is either scared or angry. If she is scared, she will attempt to rescue him by saying, "What's the matter, dear?" So now, instead of feeling depressed, he becomes angry. She, instead of feeling the fear of abandonment, feels resentful and put down and thinks to herself, "How unreasonable he is." If she is angry, she will attempt to get him to change his behavior and will persecute him by saying, "What's the matter, dear?" In this particular system, he is not allowed to be the Victim (depressed, suicidal, or sad), and through this series of transactions he becomes the angry Persecutor and she takes the Victim slot.

Different feelings can be involved, although the game may be the same. What is involved is nonacceptance. One of the couple is not allowed by the other to feel bad!

Sexy

An all-American game with couples is compulsive lover. Either one can play this game, but let's consider him. He comes from work after having had a lot of social stroking. She has been stuck in the house all day and wants adult companionship. She meets him at the door; he doesn't pay any attention to her or doesn't talk to her and she feels *rejected, put down, unappreciated.* He withdraws. Later that night, he's horny and plays sexy, and she makes it no trip or a bum trip. *He then feels hurt, rejected, and put down.* Depending on the programming he could be feeling angry or scared or sad. Meanwhile, she's feeling used or resentful, and thinking, "He doesn't love me, he uses me as a sleeping pill." Now, this can go on for five, ten, fifteen years, and then he'll wake up one morning and say to himself, "What, am I crazy!" and he'll play "no interest". After two or three weeks, she'll play "sexy" for the next fifteen years, while he plays impotent and "no interest." The gamey aspect is that he stops himself from getting what he wants, which is sex, by not being there for her when he gets home. He's not meeting her wants. When he comes home and doesn't talk to her and withdraws, she feels *hurt, rejected, and put down.* The gamey aspect on her part is that when he walks in the door, she talks to him about what the kids did, what went on at the PTA, and blasts him about what he didn't do, what he should do, etc. He feels used and thinks to himself, "What's the use? I work all day and sacrifice myself for the family and all she wants is to bang my ear." And he runs. She doesn't see that she sets it up for him to withdraw. Later at night when she rejects him, she feels his bad feelings and he feels her bad feeelings. There is a draw, a tie; nobody wins, each loses!

The funniest variation of "sexy" I have run across was with a client whose husband was self-employed. They had three small children, aged three, four, and six. He would come home in the middle of the day and make a pass at her while she was cleaning the house with the kids underfoot. She, of course, would turn him down, and later that night in bed, he would have "no interest" because she had rejected him earlier. After discussing the situation with the group, she decided that the next time he made a daytime pass at her, she would take him up on it, and if he didn't approach her, she would make advances to him.

Sure enough, one day he came home in the middle of the day, put his arm around her, and began to make sexual advances. She told him to wait while she put the three- and four-year-old kids in the backyard (the six-year-old was at school), and told them to stay there and play. She took him into the bedroom and they got undressed. She then took him into the shower with her and they scrubbed each other's backs. While they were in the shower, her next-door neighbor came into the house through the front door (it was open), and called her over and over again. They were trapped in the bathroom without clothes and waited for what seemed like hours (probably fifteen minutes) until they were sure that the neighbor left and it was safe to come out. After this incident, her husband's afternoon ardor cooled considerably; he stopped making passes at her during the day and made love to her at night. She kept her contract with the group and continued to keep after him in the afternoon and he always refused, telling her to wait. Outside of his awareness, what he had wanted in the afternoon was not to make love, but to get rejected. Incidentally, the neighbor told her later that she could see her car in front of the house, knew she was home, telephoned with no answer, had been worried, and had gone over to see if everything was all right.

About five years after this client had left the group, she and her husband came to the clinic for sex therapy. He told me he had an operation two years ago and since then had lost interest in sex. He was on medication for his heart, so I checked the medication and found that it was four times the maximum dosage recommended for his condition. One of the side effects was diminution of sexual drive. I suggested that he see another heart specialist for a second opinion on the medication. He did, and the second physician reduced the medication to within the recommended dosage, and his sex drive returned overnight.

Once in a while there's a mismatch and the holes in his head don't exactly match the rocks in hers. In this case, one of the two will fantasize a match in the other. This is to say that he doesn't see her as she really is. He sees her either as an ogress or as a saint, but not as her real self. You'll find a man who treats his wife, a charming, cultured, loving woman, as if she's some kind of horrible, vicious beast. Or you'll find some guy who thinks his wife is extremely demanding when what she actually needs is assertiveness training. Or you'll find the man who thinks his wife is superwoman, i.e., without fault but doesn't understand why he is depressed/suicidal/homicidal.

Money

One spouse plays miser and the other plays compulsive spender. In 1974 Dick gave his wife an allowance of $50 a week to clothe and feed their three children. Conservatively, the cost was about $100 a week. He was a vice-president of a large brokerage firm and had a very high income. His wife couldn't manage on $50 a week, so she would charge things; when he got the bills at the end of the month, he'd be in an uproar. Her contribution was that she would purchase things imprudently, since, regardless of how much or how little she spent, he felt it was "too much." To break up this game, he could have given her an adequate allowance.

Another client playing the same game refused to manage the checkbook, and every month would berate his wife about her spending, even though it was completely in line and she was prudent. By not handling the checkbook and the finances, he could maintain the myth that his wife was an extravagant spender. Here we have counterfeit bad feelings. This client had a tremendous need to criticize his wife. His "okay-ness" depended on her being put down.

The husband in another couple who came in for counseling couldn't care less about money, had an aversion to shopping, and kept a balance of several thousand dollars in their joint checkbook. Whenever his wife wanted to buy something, all she had to do was get it. But whenever she did buy something, he would criticize her selection.

She would try to "get him to go shopping" because she was scared she would make the wrong choice. When they needed a new living-room set, she pondered for six months, afraid to buy it, complaining to everyone about how miserable he was. Meanwhile, he wasn't even aware of what she wanted.

The resolution was for them to (agree) contract that she would go shopping and buy whatever she wanted without being concerned about her choice; he, since he didn't want to go shopping with her, would not criticize her when she bought anything.

In this one particular area, the wife put the parent face on him; that is, she responded to him as she did to her father.

Guilt and Resentment

A trade back and forth of guilt and resentment is very common in couples' relationships. If I do what I *want* to do, I feel *guilty*; if I do what *you want* me to do, I feel *resentful*. Either way, I lose.

A typical guilt-resentment scenario would go like this: He hates the opera and she loves it. He feels guilty because he hasn't taken her out in twelve years. When she says, "Let's go to the opera," he says yes because he feels guilty. They go to the opera and he now feels resentful. Outside his awareness, he drives ninety-five miles an hour to the opera house and she gets there a nervous wreck.

He sits at the opera with his stomach rumbling, belching audibly, and becoming sicker by the minute. When the performance is over, they rush out and drives home insanely. He's made it a lousy evening for her, and she's feeling guilty because she dragged him to the opera.

He likes fishing; she hates fishing and she gets seasick. So the next time he asks her to go fishing (he asks her only because he's feeling guilty; he doesn't really want her to go), she says yes. As soon as they get to the ocean, she turns green, throws up all over the boat, and they have to go back home. So she makes it a lousy day for him.

Having spent forty-six years feeling depressed and guilty before curing myself, and knowing how desperately many clients wish to overcome these feelings, I am saddened at the inability of many therapists to "cure" people of depression, guilt, anxiety, resentment, and the like. In doing group therapy, I find that fifteen to twenty-five weeks is usually enough to crack even the toughest guilt-ridden, depressed, anxious shell of clients' programming. The following clinical case illustrates the process involved in curing guilt.

Anna, aged forty-five, historically felt very angry in her marriage. She ridiculed her husband, put him down, nagged him; he, in return, persecuted her by always being absent, physically or mentally, and withdrawing from her. She came into group because she was having an affair and was feeling guilty. After the affair began, however, she had become a much better wife, more loving and accepting.

(Edited from tape):

Anna: I would like to stop feeling guilty. I am always feeling guilty. I make myself feel guilty at the drop of a hat, like it's my fault for everything that goes wrong.

Shep: Get the feeling of guilt in your current experience. When's the last time you felt guilty? Get the feeling.

Anna: I'm having an affair and I feel very guilty. My sex life with my husband Bob is lousy. He doesn't talk to me, he doesn't make love to me. He's more concerned with going out on his boat and fishing than being with me. I don't think we've had sex four times in the last year. I was very angry at him. About six months ago he had to go out of town for three weeks and I happened to meet somebody at the office where I work. We see each other once or twice a week now. And I feel really great when I'm with this person, and I'm not angry at my husband that much anymore. But I keep feeling terribly guilty. My husband is a very nice person, and my friend is married and has children and I have children, and I don't want to break up my marriage. I'm not willing to give up my boyfriend. I think it's the only thing that's keeping me sane.

Shep: Get the feeling of guilt and stay with it. What's the thought that goes with that feeling?

Anna: I'm hurting my husband.

Shep: Stay with the feeling of guilt. When did you feel that, when you were in your 30's?

Anna: Oh, when I was in my 30's I felt guilty because I made my husband go on vacation to San Francisco, and he wanted to go to Canada and go fishing, and I hate it up there. It's primitive, it's outhouses and mosquitoes, and I get bored out of my skull. I finally put my foot down and made him take me to San Francisco, and I felt very guilty.

Shep: Frankly, you don't have the power to make him take you to San Francisco. But stay with the feeling of guilt, even though you don't have the power to hurt him. Stay with the feeling. How did he act?

Anna: He sulked and he withdrew for months.

Shep: Stay with the feeling of guilt. When did you feel like this when you were younger, a teenager?

Anna: I've got it. I hurt my parents by staying out late. I used to stay out until 1:00 in the morning and I had a curfew of 11:30.

Shep: Stay with the feeling of guilt. How did you hurt your parents when you were real little?

Anna: Well, when I was in grade school I hurt my mother by not getting A's. I was always a poor student.

Shep: What would your mother do when you came home with a bad mark?

Anna: She used to yell and scream at me. She said I was killing her.

Shep: Stay with the feeling of guilt. What is the earliest memory you have?

Anna: When I was four years old my mother had an heirloom vase and I broke it.

Shep: Be four years old. You just broke the vase. What's happening?

Anna:	My mother is furious. She's yelling at me. "You rotten kid, you're no good. You're bad." Oh, she's beating me with a strap.
Shep:	Stay with it. Did you break it on purpose?
Anna:	No, it was so pretty I wanted to take it down and play with it.
Shep:	Mother is beating you with a strap. What do you decide?
Anna:	I decide I'm bad and it's not safe to play with something that Momma doesn't approve of.
Anna:	(Starts to laugh) Yeah, I married my mother and now I'm playing with something she wouldn't approve of. (Laughs)
Shep:	See yourself four years old. What do you want to tell that little girl?
Anna:	You're not bad, honey. You're entitled to play and be happy.
Shep:	There's more to it than that. Somehow you've been hypnotized to believe that you have the magic power of hurting people if you do what you want to do. You said, "I hurt my mother by breaking her vase." Be your mother and beat little Anna with the strap. And I want to talk to your mother. Role play.
Anna:	(Yelling) "You rotten kid," (wham) "give you" (wham). "I told you to stay out of there" (wham). "Don't you ever listen to me?!" (wham)
Shep:	How are you feeling, Mama?
Anna:	I feel angry and powerful.
Shep:	Be little Anna. How do you feel?
Anna:	I hurt and I'm terrified, like she's going to kill me.
Shep:	So when you were four years old you didn't hurt your mother, your mother hurt you. Is that right?
Anna:	Yes.
Shep:	And when you were a teenager, mother would come and yell and scream at you. Be your Mama.
Anna:	"It's 1:00. I told you to be in the house by 11:30. Just for that, you're not going to go out for the rest of the week. You lousy, rotten kid."
Shep:	How do you feel, Mama?
Anna:	I feel strong and powerful.
Shep:	How do you feel, Anna?

Anna: I feel bad and I feel scared.
Shep: So you didn't have the magic power to hurt Mom.
Anna: No.
Shep: Be your husband and sulk. What are you thinking and feeling, Bob.
Anna: (as Bob) I'm really mad at her. I don't want to go to San Francisco. I want to go fishing. I like to be alone. I like it up there in Canada.
Shep: So Anna, you didn't hurt your husband did you? All you did was get him angry at you.
Anna: Yes.

Strictly speaking, guilt is not a feeling. The feeling is scare and the thought is "I'm guilty." When Anna was four years old, she was guilty of breaking her mother's vase. She was sentenced to a lifetime feeling of scare with the thought, "I'm bad." As it is, Anna spent some thirty-eight years feeling guilty. Besides that, she spent thirty years overweight, angry at her husband and children, resenting them and suffering. Since beginning her affair, Anna lost twenty-five pounds. Since therapy, she gave up the guilt as well as the weight. It's possible to go through life and not give ourselves our favorite unpleasant programmed feelings of guilt or resentment.

Forgetful

Another game, a favorite of Repentant Wrongdoers, as opposed to Righteous Wrongdoers, ("Who could blame me for doing wrong when he/she did wrong."), is Forgetful. He would forget birthdays, anniversaries, holidays, etc., and she would be angry when he forgot. She wanted him to remember their anniversary and to buy her flowers and take her to dinner, the movies or a show, and be "romantic." The game went like this: He comes home on their anniversary and sees her sitting with smoke coming out of her cars. He says, "What's the matter, dear?" She says, "Ha! Do you know what today is?" He says, "Well, it's Thursday." And she says, "No, you SOB. Today is our anniversary, our twenty-sixth anniversary." He says, "Oh hell, I'm sorry, I forgot. Look, I'll buy you a corsage, take you out to dinner, and we'll go to the theater." She says, triumphantly, "If I have to remind you, forget it." Had we looked in on her an hour before he got home, we would have found her thinking triumphantly, "Wait'll he gets home and I blast him. I bet he's forgotten again this year."

The gamey aspect is that he has a computer for a brain, and remembers everything in every other area of life. He conveniently forgets anniversaries. The way to break up the game is for him to remember to have his secretary remind him, or for her to tattoo a reminder on his chest the week before, or paste it on the mirror where he shaves.

His "Forgetfulness" was evidenced in many areas. For example, he comes home, and after a brief conversation, she says, "Any normal husband would ask me how it went today. You knew I was going to the doctor." He says, "What did the doctor say?" She responds triumphantly, "If I have to remind you, forget it." This way she can hand his head to him and criticize him. He will always feel put down and think, "Oh, my God, talking to that woman is like sticking your pinkie in a pencil sharpener." She can feel justifiable anger and think, "Look at that SOB, he doesn't take any interest in me. He doesn't even care if the doctor said I have a fatal disease."

She was unwilling to abandon her position that she was "okay" and all she had to do was get *him* to change. After twenty-six years, the marriage broke up.

In doing couples' counseling, my philosophy is that since nuts come in pairs and they choose each other, I consider myself successful if I get them to work together to improve the relationship and to be happy, loving, warm, touching, and intimate. I consider that I should make significant inroads within eight weeks of counseling. The couples we see usually come to us out of desperation. I am amazed that people will live quiet lives of despair for years and years rather than go for counseling. Men particularly avoid therapy; it seems their macho is diminished. They take better care of their car than they do of their marriage. They seem to think that all emotional problems can be solved with their head and are constantly doing head jobs on themselves.

I also consider the counseling successful if, in a very damaging relationship, the couple separate and go their own ways, instead of staying together and torturing each other.

Failure is when I'm ineffective in facilitating change, either for improvement in or for dissolution of the relationship.

I very seldom advise a couple new to counseling to separate, and then only where there is severe pathology or tissue damage; i.e., somebody looks as if he or she is going to take a beating or wind up in the insane asylum; or the system is destroying the children—for example, when one of the parents is a child abuser or a child molester, and is *unwilling to change.*

Couples who separate will go out and find a clone of their previous spouse, unless they change their programming. The woman who is married to an alcoholic will divorce him and marry another alcoholic, then divorce him and marry a paranoid schizophrenic or some other type, who will be beastly to her. For this reason, I often advise clients who have just left a horrendous marriage or love affair, that if they meet someone who really turns them on, to hit the person in the head with a rock (gently, no tissue damage, please) and run.

When I am giving a lecture, very often someone will ask me, "Will my coming into an awareness group break up my marriage?" I reassure the person that a ten-week awareness course will not break up the unhappy marriage. The worse the marriage, the stronger the fear of abandonment that binds the couple together. Although in about half of the clinical examples that follow, the end result was the dissolution of the marriage, this does not occur in actual practice. Most marriages are improved with awareness and with counseling; the interesting ones are always the worst. To put it differently, the worst marriages have the most drama and provide the most human interest.

Courtroom

Marriage counseling can be a game itself, "courtroom," with the therapist cast in the role of the judge; the game can go on for years. In the typical game of "courtroom," the vocal spouse will complain for forty-five minutes about what an inconsiderate monster the other is, and the quiet spouse sits in the foxhole wearing a helmet while the heavy shelling goes on. Then when the latter has a chance, usually ten minutes before the hour is over, he/she will pop up and say, "Look how crazy my spouse is," and flop back into his/her hole. This is supposed to be therapeutic, but it isn't. Usually I allow the couple to play "courtroom" for one session and then confront them and explain the game.

Look How Hard I'm Trying

The second major game played in counseling of couples is "look how hard I'm trying," where one spouse wants to change and the other is unwilling. The unwilling one usually is also afraid to say what it is that he's thinking, i.e., fear of abandonment, and just comes so that "Mommy" won't throw him out of the house, to show her what a "good boy" he is. This game can drag on for years. The worst case I heard of was that of a therapist and his wife who, before getting a divorce, went to a world-famous therapist once a week for five years. The person who is playing "look how hard I'm trying" may be coming only so that he can leave the marriage guilt-free. At least in this case, he will leave eventually.

I counter "look how hard I'm trying" by giving couples assignments to do at the very first session, assignments they can either do or not do. Typical assignments are massaging each other or cuddling each other, or fighting with each other or not fighting with each other—something they can do!

I recently gave a workshop for social workers and psychologists. In twenty minutes, I got a couple to volunteer to go out dancing one evening a week, to massage each other, and to have sex three times a week. One analytically trained therapist asked, "What do you do about his unconscious hostility?" I told him, "If I can get the couple to be happy, enjoy being together, and have fun, I'll worry about his unconscious hostility later."

The following clinical cases abstracted from tape represent vignettes of long term "gamey" relationships.

Ernie and Muriel

Another client, Ernie, was sent to me by a major sex clinic. He couldn't get an erection. Muriel, his wife, was constantly angry, hostile, and critical of him. In working with him, he relived early scenes in which his mother had physically abused him as an infant. He had urinated in her face when she was changing his diaper, and she pinched his penis. When he was ill at the age of three and had thrown up, she squeezed his testicles. In the regression, he writhed in agony on the floor. It was horrible to see. His mother also molested him by having him perform cunnilingus on her when he was three years old. In his sex with Muriel, he ejaculated without having an erection while he performed orally on her. She did not reciprocate during oral sex!

In therapy Ernie made great changes. He became much more assertive, changed jobs, and doubled his income in six months. At a therapy marathon, he was able to crack his programming; that is, he had managed a satisfactory erection. Muriel was very unhappy with his therapy. She came to group therapy for three weeks* and just sat knitting. She was "okay"; her only problem was him. Finally, she opened up at one session and played martyr about the terrible life she'd spent with him, wept, and then never came back! This was her second marriage; her first husband had been an alcoholic, a beast. In her second marriage, Muriel became the beast. When Ernie would have an erection in his sleep, she would wake him up and force his penis into her dry vagina, guaranteeing he'd lose the erection immediately. But when he began to respond to therapy and have normal erections, she began to feel "tortured" or would not be "in the mood." He had not cracked his fear of abandonment, and when she threatened to leave him unless he quit group therapy, he caved in and left the group, returning to suffering. Not all cases are successes.

Debbie and Charlie

Debbie was very plain looking, thirty-two, employed, cultured, intellectual, a college graduate and married to Charlie, a boor. They had absolutely nothing in common; what held them together was fear of abandonment. She was nonorgasmic and came into therapy in a state of shock because she had caught Charlie cheating *again*. She had caught him twice before, and his excuse was her inability to experience orgasm. He had promised her he would never cheat again, but he did. They had no children because "he didn't want any."

What made Charlie pick a nonorgasmic woman and keep

---

*On a different night than the night Ernie came. I did not think it advisable to have them in the same group. I usually like to have couples in the same group together.

her that way? He was at first reluctant to come with her for sex therapy, but finally agreed. He came for two sessions and would not do any of the assignments. He wanted to have a nonorgasmic wife who would stay at home so he could be the Child. For the first eight years of their marriage, she had been in the Parent slot: angry, hostile, and critical. However, she had given up hope of changing him and getting angry at him and was now deeply depressed, scared, and having anxiety attacks. Since there was no way to salvage the marriage and because he categorically refused to do anything to improve their relationship, she came in for individual and group therapy and worked on changing herself. She developed social skills so that she could meet men with the hope of finding a warm and loving relationship. She found a man, had an affair, and had an orgasm! She then divorced Charlie; today she is happier as a single than she was when she was married.

Jack and Jill

Outside of her awareness, Jill was phobic and had a fear of being with people and of going out dancing and doing new things. In her awareness, she thought she wanted to be out having fun. Jack was a stay-at-home stick-in-the-mud. In this particular relationship, Jack was the Child and Jill was in the Parent slot. She was his Mommy. On the rare occasions when she could get Jack to go out, he had a great time. Jill, on the other hand, did not enjoy herself. Jack was a corporate executive and traveled, but would always come home for the weekends and stay at home, depressed and withdrawn. If he wasn't depressed, he'd work around the house gardening, remodeling the attic, putting up siding, keeping himself busy, and keeping away from Jill. They both assumed that Jack kept her from going out and meeting people and exploring places. In reality, Jack was rescuing Jill from her phobias and taking care of her need to be kept at home. Meanwhile, he was taking all the heat, by also taking care of her programmed need to be angry. Jill could stay safely at home and blame him for not taking her out. Instead of going out and feeling abandoned and alone, Jack felt depressed and withdrawn. And, of course, they blamed each other.

Jack persecuted Jill from the Victim slot; she persecuted him from the Persecutor slot. However, they took turns! Jack was very thrifty and when he was out of town and Jill was alone and depressed, she would buy expensive clothing and jewelry to lift her spirits. When he got back, he usually switched roles; he became hypercritical and would persecute her from the Persecutor position, while she played Victim, saying, "Of course I bought a new dress; I was so depressed" (Righteous Wrongdoer). This would infuriate Jack further. What he wanted her to be was a Repentant Wrongdoer, and say, "I'm sorry, I'm sorry!" After blowing his stack, Jack could withdraw and sulk, instead of being depressed. Anger mobilizes, so he would dive into some kind of activity which would get Jill feeling abandoned, and then the system would recycle.

Therapy with this couple consisted of getting Jack to take Jill out more often and talk to her and spend time with her, instead of withdrawing and working around the house. He was to give her compliments instead of being critical. In return, Jill stopped her impulsive spending and had more sex with Jack, which is what he wanted.

Of course, Jill also eventually got in touch with her fears of new people and places and dealt with them.

Rudy and Trudy

Trudy came into therapy in the Parent slot. She was fifty-five, had been married to Rudy for thirty-five years, and had never had an orgasm. Their two children were grown and living away from home. Rudy insisted on sex, after which she would become depressed and suicidal.

Trudy worked through her depression and then brought Rudy in for marriage counseling, which was ineffective. He would not change. He worked long hours in the city (a two-hour commute), and was gone twelve to fourteen hours a day. They ended the marriage counseling and Trudy felt okay, so she stopped coming to group therapy.

After three years, Trudy came back for group and individual therapy and raised her self-esteem to a point where she was considering having an affair. For eight or nine years she had been flirting with a married man who worked in her office. She went to a motel with him and reported it was a horrifying experience.

She was terrified and screamed when he entered her! She scared the devil out of him, and they both ran out of the motel! A week later they went back to the motel, and she had her first orgasm at age fifty-eight! I remember her coming into the office, looking like a teenager, her face glowing, and saying with delight, "I'm not frigid. I'm not frigid." She left Rudy, got her own apartment, and had several affairs. But she didn't like the singles scene and didn't find anybody compatible.

She went back with Rudy, and the relationship greatly improved because she could have orgasms. Their sex life was excellent and when I last heard, they were having sex almost every night. This, incidentally, raised Rudy's self-esteem, which had also been very low. They resolved his problem of his working in the city by moving into the city so they could have more time together and enjoy each other's company.

John and Laurie

Laurie was married for twenty-five years, wishing her husband would drop dead. During her marriage, Laurie fantasized having an affair and getting away from him. She was angry, hostile, and critical, and he was depressed and withdrawn. She took my ten-week course to *learn how to change* her husband, rather than to develop awareness for herself, and left. Two years later, she returned in a complete state of shock. Her husband had come home one night and told her he had a younger woman and was moving out. She said, "Should I let him go?" I said, "Well, you have no choice; he's gone." After losing her husband, Laurie picked up the pieces and made big changes in herself and met John. He was a lovable guy, and they had a beautiful relationship. During six months of courtship, they rented a house and moved in together.

Soon John and Laurie came back for couples counseling and they said, "Gee, when we're out together, we have a wonderful time and have lots of fun, but the minute we walk into the house, it's like the shades were pulled down. We're both quiet, withdrawn, sad." I asked Laurie what it was like in her house when she was little; she said, "Nobody ever made noise or had fun." I asked John the same question and he gave the same answer as Laurie. I said, "So, going home means being quiet and not having any fun. Now what can you do to make noise and have fun when you're in the house together?" With awareness, they very rapidly changed.

Unless we have awareness and make deliberate conscious efforts to change, we will bring our programming with us to our coupling/marriage.

Beauty and the Beast

Beauty and the Beast had a miserable marriage. Beauty was referred to me by her family physician. Her husband was always angry and controlled the family—his wife and their two sons—with his anger. He terrorized them.

Eventually Beast had a heart attack and was at home all the time. Now there was no escaping him; he had all the family terrified, telling them they were killing him any time they did something he didn't like. Of course, his family weren't killing him and he himself was responsible for his anger, but he had the whole family in an enormous game of "blackmail." Because of his miserable behavior, Beast drove Beauty to the verge of a nervous breakdown. In three weeks of therapy, she was to the point where she would withdraw from him and tell him, "I don't have to stay here and listen to your anger."

Beast could no longer terrorize Beauty with his anger, he got in touch with his fear of abandonment and became a pussycat. His pussycat behavior held up for about three weeks, during the time she was in therapy. He didn't want her coming to therapy, and promised to behave if she stopped our sessions. (He probably had a tremendous fear of her becoming cured.) She stopped coming to therapy, and I didn't see or hear from her for about two months. Then, all of a sudden, she was back again because he had reverted to his old self, angry, hostile and terrorizing the children.

Two weeks after Beauty returned to therapy, Beast became a pussycat again. He again promised to behave if she would again leave therapy; she stopped. I expect she'll be back, because there has been no change in the system.

Beast is afraid, and it is unfortunate that he will not come for therapy. The contract Beauty had with him was that he would behave as long as she didn't go to therapy. It might be that he's so terrified she will change that he is willing to forgo his anger. Beauty's fear of abandonment, of course, matched Beast's.

I have given one-half of this story, the wife's side. What was never brought to her awareness was the dynamics of the family system. The wife picked a man with a terrible temper, who terrorized her and her sons. I have no idea of how she persecuted him from the Victim slot, but I am sure she did.

We do therapy on a contract, or an agreement basis, in that the client sets his or her own goals. The flaw in the contract method, one that I have never resolved, is that I am powerless to keep the client in therapy once the original limited goal has been attained. I am sure that in the system just discussed the entire family needed therapy—husband, wife, sons. However, the husband would absolutely not submit to therapy, and the client's sole interest was in controlling her husband's anger.

Romeo and Juliet

Juliet, about forty-five years old, had taken an awareness course with us just after she had divorced her depressed, withdrawn husband. Juliet and her husband had a fourteen-year-old son and a sixteen-year-old daughter. Two years after her divorce, Juliet had a wild affair with a fifty-year-old school teacher who was also divorced and the father of two children, aged fifteen and seventeen.

Every night he climbed in her window, so her children wouldn't know, and made passionate love to her two or three times. Then at five in the morning, he would climb out the window and sneak back into his own house, so his children wouldn't find out he had been away all night.

Romeo and Juliet got married and bought a house together. In four months she came back into therapy. Her complaint was that Romeo sat around withdrawn and depressed and wasn't meeting her needs. Evidently in his programming he would make passionate love to mistresses but not to wives.

The games that they were playing were pushing her into a nervous breakdown. The husband's son would come into the house all hours of the day and night, play the stereo, get into fist fights with the wife's son, and make advances to her daughter, use her Mix Master to stir paint—I could go on and on. The father encouraged his wife to discipline his son, but *didn't back her up.* When the kid made a mess in the kitchen, the father would get on his case and the kid would clean it up, but the father would not discipline him or punish him. The father's major mode of disciplining was to lecture, which bounced off this kid's back like ping-pong balls against a steel wall.

Romeo's previous wife had been hospitalized for a mental disorder, had left him, and was living on the West Coast. Romeo's mother had had several nervous breakdowns. The whole family system and game was "let's drive Mom crazy." Juliet held down a full-time job, in addition to taking care of the household and the four children—the stress was unbelievable!

Juliet terminated her second marriage by getting a divorce, and moved out. Two months later, Romeo was back on her doorstep, the passionate lover, begging for another chance! Juliet came to realize that a relationship with Romeo would be good only as long as she was his "mistress," and that when he begged for another chance outside of his awareness, he meant another chance to drive her crazy! She sought my advice.

This kind of relationship is one of the few I overtly recommend termination. There have been others. I think it is important for a marriage counselor to know when a system is not going to work and that heavy damage is down the line!*

Bill and Martha

When Bill and Martha got married, they were both virgins. Martha rationalized that she had kept herself pure for her wedding. Much to her disappointment, after five years of marriage, Martha was still pure. She spent five miserable years berating Bill for his impotence.

Martha went to a therapist to get the courage to divorce Bill. Instead of bringing her and Bill together or asking her how she came to pick an impotent man, the therapist used Bill as the basically "not okay" one instead of using the concept "nuts come in pairs," and encouraged Martha to leave Bill.

---

*If psychology is a science, as psychologists claim, then as scientists they should be able to predict events, which is part of what science is all about! The ability to predict events with some degree of accuracy is essential to effective counseling.

One of the ways we can handle our "not okay-ness" is to get into a relationship where we are the parent so we don't need to deal with it. Martha got a divorce from Bill and then went into a state of shock. When she was alone in her apartment, she would shake, have anxiety attacks, and hear noises thinking that burglars were in the apartment. When she learned that all the men she dated were potent, she discovered she had an enormous fear of sex.

Martha, who had been raised on an army post, came to me on the verge of being hospitalized for a nervous breakdown. In three months, Martha got in touch with having been terrorized and abused by both her parents, who were alcoholics, and her older sisters. Because she had been sexually abused by orderlies at the army post, she had avoided relations with men and had blocked out all these memories, so that in her mind she was really a virgin. She had a tremendous fear of sex and had married an impotent man so that she could stay away from her own "not okayness." It took another year of therapy before Martha was able to relate to men.

Most marriage counseling is not as dramatic as some of the examples I've given. A more or less "par for the course" clinical case, edited from tapes, follows.

Bob and Mary—It's Never Too Late

Bob and Mary came in for a ten-week awareness course. She had literally dragged him in, and he was thoroughly enjoying it. This was getting her a little peeved. He was sixty-eight, she was sixty-four; they had been married for forty-five years. They had five grown children, twelve grandchildren, no financial problems; Bob was retired.

Bob and Mary had been childhood sweethearts and had spent a lifetime together.

The fifth week of the course, on a Wednesday night, Mary asked me to arrange for an hour of private counseling. I told them to come in that Friday morning.

Bob was thin as a rail, about six feet tall; Mary was around five feet two inches and pleasingly plump. An edited version of our session follows.

Bob: She's a very slow eater and every night at dinnertime

| | she makes me wait for my dessert. She will not give me my apple pie until she's through eating and she's ready for her dessert. |

Shep: Huh?

Bob: She's the world's slowest eater. She puts out supper and I eat my food normally and I'm ready for my apple pie and she's eating so slowly that I wait and wait and wait and she will not give me my apple pie.

Shep: (Looks at Mary and raises his eyebrows quizically.)

Mary: He wolfs down his food, eats like an animal, so fast, and then he sits there while I'm eating, glaring daggers at me with his left hand clenched in a fist and chain-smoking cigarettes. I believe dinner should be a sociable affair and people should eat together and he doesn't do this.

Shep: What about when you eat out?

Mary: If we eat out or when we eat out, he's not bad. He still eats rapidly, but it doesn't bother me.

Shep: What would you like from Bob?

Mary: I'd like Bob to eat his food like a human being, slowly, and be company at the dinner table, not sit there and glare at me like a wild animal.

Shep: He always eats apple pie?

Mary: Every night. He's a thickheaded stubborn Irishman, as obstinate as they come, and the only time he doesn't eat apple pie is if we happen to be at a catered dinner and it isn't on the menu. And potatoes—if he doesn't have potatoes with his supper, he doesn't consider it a meal. Meat, potatoes, and apple pie, that's all the man lives on.

Shep: (Looking at Bob) So you would like Mary to eat faster and give you your apple pie as soon as you're ready for it?

Bob: (Nods yes)

Shep: (Looking at Mary) And you would like Bob to eat slower and not glare at you during dinner and wait until you're ready to serve him his apple pie.

Mary: (Nods yes)

Shep:	How do you feel, Bob, when Mary doesn't give you your apple pie?
Bob:	Resentful.
Shep:	How do you feel, Mary, when Bob sits there glaring at you?
Mary:	Angry.
Shep:	Bob, I have a hunch that what's going on in your head is that you're thinking "if she really loved me, she'd give me my apple pie now."
Bob:	(Nods his head yes.)
Shep:	(Looking at Mary) And I have a hunch that what's going on in your head is "if you really loved me, you'd eat slower and not glare at me and not want apple pie until I had my dessert."
Mary:	(Nods her head)
Shep:	(Looking at Bob) If Mary gave you your apple pie right away, would you be willing to sit and keep her company and not glare?
Bob:	Yes.
Shep:	(To Mary) If you were to give Bob his apple pie right away at supper, what would you like in exchange from Bob, some behavior that you dislike that you would like him to do less of or something that you like that he does that you would like him to do more of?
Mary:	I would like him when we're in the car to drive sensibly. He drives like a maniac and I always get upset with him when we go in the car any place.
Shep:	(To Mary) I can understand how this can be very upsetting.
Bob:	I don't drive recklessly, although at times I do drive fairly fast. I have been driving since I was nineteen years old and I've never had an accident.
Mary:	Oh, yeah, what about last January?
Bob:	That wasn't my fault.
Shep:	Oh, hold it, hold it. Let's work on driving and on the pie, since that's what's the issue, not about blaming. Bob, if Mary gives you your apple pie without your

	having to wait, would you be willing to drive slower?
Bob:	Yes.
Shep:	Since it seems to bother Mary very much, what would you say is "slowly?" At what speed is Mary satisfied that it's slow enough.
Bob:	There's a lot of times when Mary isn't upset when I drive and, usually, you know, I don't speed.
Shep:	(Looks at Mary) Is this true?
Mary:	Yes. If we go some place where we don't have any set time to be there or if we just go out for a ride. The only time he really drives like a maniac is when we're late to get some place.
Shep:	(To Bob and Mary) How do you arrange to be late, so Bob can get to drive like a maniac?
Mary:	I don't arrange it, he arranges it. I'm always on time, when it comes to going any place. It's true I am slow, so I get ready an hour before and he doesn't get ready until the last minute because he's so "fast," so when it's time to go, it's either he can't find his cufflinks, he can't find his tie, or he has to change his shirt because he decides he doesn't like the color. So that when it comes to going any place, I'm always waiting for him.
Shep:	(To Bob) Is this true? You're always late?
Bob:	(Smiles sheepishly) Well, I am very fast and I always figure I have plenty of time to get ready and there's no point for me to get ready an hour before we're going to go some place.
Shep:	Well, I think the problem is solvable. Let me ask you how is the marriage otherwise?
Bob:	Mary is a wonderful woman and a fine mother and a man couldn't ask for a better wife.
Mary:	We have a good marriage. Bob is a good man. He doesn't drink, he's kind and considerate, outside of his eating and driving.
Shep:	Well, I mean, like do you have fun together? Do you do things you enjoy?
Mary:	We have a good life. We both love to garden and in the summer we have the grandchildren up to visit us

	and we're active in the community and the church. We belong to a bridge club and we play bridge and I think that we've been very lucky.

Bob: (Nods his head in agreement)

Shep: Okay, so let's make contracts around the issues. A contract is something that we all agree to, so if there is anything you disagree with, you let me know and I'm going to write it down so you have a written agreement, okay? (Both nod their head okay.)

Shep: Okay. Bob is to get his apple pie whenever he wants it. As a matter of fact, will you put his apple pie on the table before you start the meal, so whenever he wants it he can just reach out and grab a chunk, even before the meal! And Bob agrees to keep you compay at the dinner table and not glare at you. Is that okay? (Both nod their heads.) Now on the driving, Bob is to drive sensibly and not speed, and it would be nice if Bob would be ready ten or fifteen minutes before you have to leave. But even if you are late, so you'll be late a few more minutes. It makes no difference. At least you'll arrive there and Mary will feel good. Are you willing to do this for Mary? And I know it will take an effort.

Bob: Yes.

Shep: Okay, and the other thing is at the dinner table, I want you, Mary, to practice eating slower, really get in touch with eating slow. So that you stretch it out another ten or fifteen minutes. Eat as slowly as you can and Bob, I want you to practice eating faster. Eat as fast as you can. And let me explain why. I know that you, Bob, would eat slower if you could, so that for some reason or other you can't slow down, and Mary would eat faster if she could but, for some reason she can't speed up, and there is no real reason for you to change if you don't want to. So, if you practice turning it on, then maybe you'll have control over it and you can turn it off if you choose to. Will you do this for one week until we meet again? (Bob and Mary both nod agreement.)

This was Friday morning. Next Wednesday evening, when they came into group, they were all smiles. Bob was eating slower, Mary was eating faster; Bob was driving slower and sensibly. They made an appointment for the following Friday. The session went as follows.

Shep: What would you like to work on?

Bob: Well, Mary nags me in the car and she backseat-drives, and I wish she wouldn't.

Shep: Have you told Mary about this or asked her to stop backseat-driving?

Bob: No.

Shep: How do you feel when she nags?

Bob: Resentful.

Shep: (To Mary) It seems as if Bob doesn't express his anger and turns it into resentment. How does he get you to nag him in the car?

Mary: Well, he either gets lost when he knows the way or he goes through stop signs.

Shep: How long have you been backseat-driving?

Mary: (Laughs) Thirty years, forty years.

Shep: Has it done any good?

Mary: No.

Shep: So what's telling him going to do? Will you make a contract to just ignore his going through stop signs and getting lost, stop rewarding him for doing this?

Mary: Yes.

Shep: What would you want from Bob in return for your not naggging him?

Mary: I would like him to talk to me more and to tell me how he feels. All he does is clam up.

Shep: I suspect that he just doesn't express disagreement in general. Is that true?

Mary: Yes.

Shep: I'm going to give you an assignment that you may think ridiculous, but I think it is very important. I would like you every day for five to ten minutes to set aside a particular time to argue. Mary, you're to dump on Bob whatever accumulated stuff you have, and Bob is to have ten minutes to express any resentment he has. Now, Bob, instead of being critical, the

way to do this is to say, "I feel _____ that you
_____." So like you would say, "I feel *very
angry* (or resentful) when you *tell me how to drive.*"
What I am not hearing is arguments. I would like you
to argue with each other ten minutes a day rather than
hold it in and take it out other ways.

Comment: Both Bob and Mary agreed to this and returned to
group, when they reported they had nothing to argue about.
Bob said that when he did verbalize something, it sounded so
trivial to him that he laughed about it. Very often, there are no
major problems in a marriage. However, very minor itty-bitty
problems can be extremely irritating over a long period. The
precipitating factor in Bob and Mary's coming in to take the
course was that when Bob was working, he was out of the house
most of the time. Now that he was retired, he was at home most
of the time and they had more time to irritate each other. Prac-
tically all the games they played were played around hurrying up
and slowing down and withdrawing and not expressing resentment, and Mary coming on Rescuer or Persecutor. The work
they did, as described above, contributed to their awareness and
the break up of the games.

I have spent a lot of time on this chapter, reemphasizing the
process with numerous clinical cases because we choose partners
with a programming that complements our own, and often remain in tormented and tormenting marriages because of our
fear of abandonment. No matter how you look at it, nuts come
in pairs.

Do-It-Yourselfers

If you want to improve your relationship, the first thing I
recommend is massage. An excellent book on the subject is
George Downing's *The Massage Book* (Random House, New
York, 1975) available through your local bookstore.

Usually one of the first assignments I give a couple is to start
massaging each other. I tell them it is no fun learning, which will
take two weeks, in which time they will not enjoy massaging,
but after this period they will enjoy the activity and it will have
great beneficial effects. I recommend massage for many
reasons.

1. Some men have the adolescent idea that touch equals sex,

but it doesn't. Some people have acquired a "don't touch" message from their parents. On the contrary, in a warm, loving relationship, touch is extremely important. An infant doesn't come out of his mother's womb not wanting to be touched. A couple who will not touch each other physically have very little hope of touching each other emotionally!

2. The next thing I do is have the couple make up a list of what the one desires of the other. He writes, "Our relationship would be better if she would _____." She writes, "Our relationship would be better if he would _____." I then have them read the statement to each other and check out if it applies to them. For example, if the man writes, "Our relationship would be better if my wife was more considerate," I will ask her if this is true. She can say yes or no. Then I'll ask him to read that over and substitute "I" instead of "she"—"if I were more considerate."

Very often what we want from the other person is something we are not giving that person. It is important that the want be reduced to terms that are understandable to a seven-year-old, and that they be put in behavioral form! For example, she says, "Our relationship would be better if he would listen to me." I will ask her what would he be doing if he were listening to her? She says, "He would understand my feelings." I reply, "What would he be doing if he was understanding your feelings? How would I, as an outside observer, know?" She may answer, "If he understood my feelings, he wouldn't leave his socks around." So, what she would like is for him not to be a slob. In other words, it has to be specific behavioral things that both can do. Once this is established, we then bargain. "Are you willing to pick up your socks if she makes you lasagna once a week? Are you will to make lasagna once a week if he will clean out the garage?" And so forth. Determine each other's wants, and then, one step at a time, make a specific behavior change.

3. This is a restatement of statement 2: "What does your spouse do that you like, that you would want more of; and what does your spouse do that you dislike, that you would like less of?" These requests, again, should be operationally defines. Then they have to be negotiated so that there's mutual agreement.

4. I work to break up the repetitive transactions that wind up with bad feelings. This has been illustrated elsewhere.

5. On the feeling level, I explore with the couple how each got to like these favorite bad feelings. Where did they get the hand-me-down? And for you, the reader, I suggest you review Chapter 7 on Role Modeling.

Once the couple is in touch with what each one wants, how each has been programmed to feel bad, and what games they are playing, and start massaging each other, the chances are they'll increase their lovemaking and be more loving. Usually when people are shown the road, they will go the path by themselves.

CHAPTER 14

And Then There Were Three

I have had no formal training in family therapy, but I am interested in all types of therapy. When I occasionally read a book or material on family therapy, I was puzzled by the unclear concepts, the classifications, and the methodologic approach. It seems that the less known about a subject, the longer it takes to explain it!

I started doing family therapy on my own—that is, have families come if for sessions—and after a few years I found that what I was doing was highly successful. Almost every family I saw changed in a relatively short time; four, five, six, seven, eight sessions.

The problem for me was how to train others to do what I was doing when I had no model or paradigm. One day in 1976 I sat down and tried to figure out what I was doing. I was not sure just what it was I was doing that made my method effective, and how I could explain it. Suddenly a light bulb went on, and I thought of the Pied Piper of Hamelin. As a model or paradigm, the original story of the Pied Piper illustrates a common pattern I had been observing while doing family therapy, in which one spouse is withdrawn, missing physically or psychologically; and the other is getting his or her needs met in an unhealthy and unhappy way through the children. Superimposed on this broad pattern are specific think/feel/act patterns handed down by previous generations.

In the fable, the people of the medieval town of Hamelin, being persecuted by hordes of rats, appeal to their Lord Mayor for help. He hires an itinerant flute player, the Pied Piper, to get rid of the rats. The Mayor and Piper argue about payment, and finally the Mayor agrees to pay the Piper an exhorbitant sum (in the Mayor's mind) in gold, should the Piper be successful.

The Piper, who has the ability to enchant any creature into following him by playing irresistible tunes, succeeds in luring the rats into the river, where they drown. The Mayor then refuses to pay the agreed price and offers the Piper a token payment. The Piper, burning with resentment for having been cheated, lures the children of the town into following him inside a magic mountain, where he and they disappear forever.

The townspeople spend the rest of their lives mourning for the missing children. The fable ends with the rumor that somewhere in Transylvania lives a community of blond children (Transylvanians are all dark haired; Hamelinians are blond) with an itinerant flute player.

Nothing more is said of the Lord Mayor of Hamelin, who probably spend the rest of his life as Mayor, hated and feared by the people; nor are we told of the life of the Piper, a creative and talented artist, now doomed to be nursemaid to some hundred-odd children.

The Pied Piper, to some degree, is the recurrent pattern of all or almost all families coming into therapy. Roles are interchangeable, and either spouse can pay or play the Piper. For illustration, the husband (Lord Mayor) promises an amount in gold (love, affection, security) to the wife (Piper) if she will get rid of the rats (his fears of abandonment, rejection, anxieties, and the like). He does not deliver the gold (he cannot satisfy her need for security or allay her childhood fears of abandonment, rejection, anxieties, and the like), and in real life, she is unable to get rid of the rats (his unresolved childhood issues). She, in turn, feeling cheated, steals the children as payment (seeks to have her needs met by the children). The children cannot meet her unresolved childhood needs any more than her spouse could. In turn, their need to be allowed to be themselves, that is, children, is not met. No one's needs to be loved, close, intimate, and joyful have been met.

What I was doing was changing the existing Pied Piper patterns, getting the parents to meet each other's needs, and freeing the children, using the following procedures:

1. Establish how all members of the family contribute to the presenting problem.

2. Determine and diagram the hand-me-downs (feeling and behavior patterns) for each member of the family. These patterns should be traced back one or more generations to eliminate the possibility of any member of the family blaming himself, herself, or his or her parents.

3. Establish each member of the family as a Victim and have him or her describe his or her bad feelings so as to avoid blame. ("I feel angry when_____," rather than, "She makes me angry because_____"), and draw a Victim triangle or triangles.

4. Contract* to get the Victim's needs met, so as to break up the harmful family patterns.

This pattern is easily identifiable in many families; for example:

• The spouse of the alcoholic or workaholic male usually plays the Piper. On occasion, Mom will play crazy or sick, and the workaholic gets stuck playing Piper.

• In the abused-child family, the abuser usually is the Piper. The abuser gives the child warmth, love, affection. When the child wants to be left alone or wishes not to be controlled, the abuser sees this as rejection and gives the child bruises, broken bones, and tissue damage. Usually the spouse is aloof. This may explain why some abused children seem to have an enormous investment in protecting the abusing parent—he or she is their only source of nurturing.

• In the schizophrenia-producing family, the Piper is extremely controlling and close to the child. Very often one member of

---

*"Contract" means, to assign or negotiate goals involving behavior and/or feeling changes that are mutually agreeable to the involved parties, therapist and family members.

the family, usually a parent, is highly rational and unfeeling and does the thinking for the schizophrenic member, who is not rational and who does the feeling for both of them. The Piper takes care of the child and actively prevents the child from taking care of himself or herself. This pattern may also be that of the family which produces a child who is obese or emaciated (anorexia nervosa).

• In the one-parent family, either an older child or a grandmother is forced to play Piper while the parent plays Lord Mayor (usually the father or the working mother). This pattern is also common in the family in which a spouse has deserted the family.

• In the family where both parents work, an older child may be trained to play Piper, while both parents take turns as Lord Mayor.

• In the family producing a sociopath or psychopath, both parents abandon parenthood (Piper and Lord Mayor roles) and assume Child roles. This type of family will seldom, if ever, be seen by the family therapist. Such a family is familiar, however, to social case workers.

Many variations of the patterns just discussed are possible; for example:

• Both parents may take on the Lord Mayor role and hire a surrogate Piper, that is, a nursemaid or a governess. Having abandoned parenting does not mean the parents are necessarily distant from each other. Later, when the children are older, the parents will use a boarding school to play the Piper role, and still later a mental hospital or a psychotherapist.

• In some families both parents play Piper, in an intense struggle to get their needs met by the children. The children are caught in the middle of a tug of war.

• Sometimes one parent may play Piper to one child and Lord Mayor to another. Although there are countless variations, the process in all troubled families is similar.

Individual Patterns: Hand-Me-Downs

Parents will have think/feel/act patterns that are handed down to them from previous generations. Within their awareness, parents do not usually see themselves as having those characteristics they disliked in their parents, although actually they often are just like their parents.

As described elsewhere, one child will be trained to be compliant, one rebellious, one just like Uncle Willie, who came to a bad end at an early age, and so forth. If Dad has a need to be angry and scared, one child will be trained to get him angry, one to scare him, and one to despair him.

Using the Pied Piper as a model, I found that in one week I could train therapists who were experienced in working with individuals and couples to work with families. In that week they had a working model for family therapy, could make a beginning, and with a little experience could do effective therapy. It's really remarkable how clear family therapy becomes.

In the stereotype of the American family, dad is cast in the role of Persecutor, Mom as Rescuer, and the children as Victims. For example, Mom tells Dad what the kids have done, Dad persecutes them, Mom then persecutes Dad by telling him that he is too hard on the children, and rescues the children by giving them cookies after Dad has sent them to bed without supper. (This was the case in my own family system when I was growing up.) Later the kids will persecute Mom by failing in school, drinking, using drugs, becoming pregnant, getting arrested, or at least coming home at three or four in the morning. Family members readily see each other as Persecutors and themselves as Victims. They are, however, not so ready to see themselves as Persecutors or to see how they persecute the other family members. Bringing this into their awareness and removing blame is of prime importance.

The following clinical case is an illustration of the procedures I use in family therapy:

The father, aged fifty-two, is a successful small businessman. He has a shop with four employees and does special model building for aerospace electronics corporations. His customers use him rather than their own personnel; moreover, he has a reputation for expertise. He works seventy hours a week "trying" to catch up with his backlog. The mother, aged forty-seven, is an attractive, well-groomed woman, with an extraordinary personality and sense of humor.

She had taken the awareness course and everyone in group was attracted to her. The son is a young thirteen, that is prepuberty.

Mother (M), father (F), and son (S) enter the room. Mother and son sit on the couch, with the father sitting opposite them on the other side of the room. At the mother's insistence they have come for family counseling. The transcript of the interview appears in the left column, and a discussion and comments are in the right column.

Edited Transcript of Family Interview	Comments
Shep: What brought you here?	I began this particular interview by looking at the ceiling instead of any family member. Instead of addressing myself to a specific person, I just wanted to see what would happen and who would respond.
M: (After twenty-second silence) The problem is our son. He gets angry and calls me names when I try to get him to wear his rubbers, do his homework, come home at a reasonable hour, clean his room, or take a bath.	
Shep: How do you feel when he calls you names?	
M: I feel hurt and rejected. I get a knot in my stomach.	I determine Mom's bad feelings and identify her as a Victim. The knot in her stomach is scare and resentment. On a nonverbal level, I let her know that I am kind and sympathetic and will help her.
Shep: What do you do to get your son angry and call you names?	Since Mom is highly motivated and brought the family into therapy, she is confronted first. The rest of the family is reassured when they hear how Mom contributes.
M: Nothing.	
F: Tell him.	Dad won't let her get away with it. Actually he barked "Tellum!"

Edited Transcript of Family Interview	Comments
M: (Smiles) He says I nag him.	Outside her awareness, Mom smiles at this point. Very often when we are in programmed behavior (behavior that in our awareness we hate), outside our awareness there is a deep visceral comfort, and we smile. If I had confronted Mom with her smile, she probably would have said, "If I wasn't smiling, I'd be crying."

Just then the son sniffles. Mom says, "Blow your nose." The son coughs, looks at the therapist, and says, "That's psychosomatic, Doc." (In the space of a few seconds, a whole pattern becomes obvious.)

Shep: (To son) Been to the doctor?	
S: Yeah, lots of doctors. I have a psychosomatic cough.	
Shep: How do you feel when Mom takes you to lots of doctors?	
S: Lousy. She is always after me.	Establishes the son as a Victim and determines his bad feelings. Nonverbally, I let the son know by nodding in agreement that I understood and sympathized.
Shep: (To Mom) Seems to me you take care of your son. Who did you take care of when you were little?	
M: My mother was always sick. I used to take care of her.	
Shep: Ah, so your Mom was in the business of being sick, so she trained you to take care of her. Needing someone to take care of, you trained your son to be sick.	This is very important, because it indirectly tells Mom that she was trained to be a caretaker. The implication is that she can change. It also puts responsibility on her for training her son to be sick. By placing the responsibili-

Edited Transcript of Family Interview	Comments

ty on her, the hope is that she will be able to stop training her son to be sick.

(As I say this to Mom, I draw the following diagram on the blackboard, so the family can see it. Figure 5)

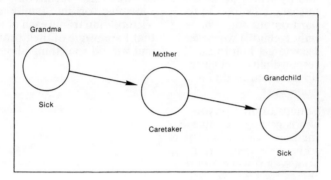

Figure 5

Shep:	(To Mom) Who trained Grandma to be sick when she was young?	We have already blamed Mom, and to take some of the heat off her, we go back a step in the generational pattern and blame Grandma.
M:	Nobody. She was run over by a runaway horse and wagon when she was little, and for years she couldn't get around.	
Shep:	So a chance accident trained her. Who did you take care of before you had your son?	I determine and diagram the hand-me-downs for each member of the family. Establishing generational patterning removes guilt and blame. The implication is, "You don't have to wear them (hand-me-downs) for the rest of your life."
M:	Oh, I took care of my husband's office, his books, the masses. I was a member of the Young Peoples Socialist League.	

	Edited Transcript of Family Interview	Comments

Shep: The caretaker ends up persecuted. How do you get persecuted?

M: My son persecutes me by not taking care of himself and by yelling at me. My husband tells me I'm too hard on our son ("he is only a child") whenever I try to get him to take responsibility and clean up his room or do his homework.

Comment: Up to now, the father and son have not seen themselves as Persecutors. By identifying each member of the family as a Victim, I am telling each of them that I am aware of their problem and will do something about it.

Shep: Sounds to me like your son is getting a double message from each of you to be dependent. From you, Mom, when you do things for him, like tell him to blow his nose, clean his room, etc., and from you, Dad, when you tell Mom he is only a boy when Mom tries to get him to take responsibility for himself. You have much of a childhood, Dad?

F: No, my father died when I was eleven and I became the man of the house. I went to work when I was fourteen. I never had a childhood.

Comment: Dad had been sitting stiff as a board, sour and dour, gruff, serious, and unsmiling. His answer is not unexpected.
Here I establish Dad as a Victim and determine his programming and bad feelings.

Shep: Still working hard?

F: Yes, I have my own business.

M: He works seventy hours a week. He's never home, and I'm left with all the responsibilities.

Comment: Since Dad squealed on Mom earlier, she is now squealing on him.

Shep: (To Dad) Was your father a hard worker?

Edited Transcript of Family Interview	Comments

F: Yes, he was never home.
He died of a heart attack.

Heavy issues, such as Dad may be killing himself working, are not gone into until later in therapy.

Shep: How do you feel when
Mom gets after your son?

(I draw the following diagram, Figure 6.)

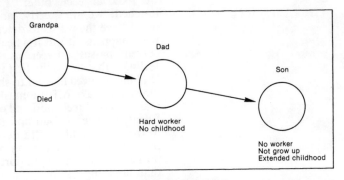

Figure 6
Hand-Me-Downs

F: I feel, "My God, why can't she leave the kid alone?

A thought, not a feeling.

Shep: Angry? Despair? Sad?
What goes with it?

F: When she goes on and on, I get nervous and angry. Once in a while I yell at the kid, but most of the time I just sit and eat my kishkes.

"Eat my kishkes" is Dad's way of saying he feels burning resentment. Literally, "Eat my own guts."

Shep: Seems to me you would like your son to have the childhood you were deprived of.

F: Yes (sighs deeply.)

The deep sigh indicates paydirt. Dad has never gotten over the hurt of having lost his childhood.

Edited Transcript of
Family Interview

Comments

Shep: The feeling of anger
and despair, is that an old
familiar feeling?

F: Very. (Said with great
emphasis. For the first
time, Dad now be-
comes alive.)

Dad has been feeling anger
and despair since he was
eleven years old. These are
his programmed feelings. I now
know I have Dad with me, and
we look at each other. I am
touched; we sit quietly, and I
don't have the words to describe
what happens. It's as if a healing
current passes between us. My
feeling is that this is the first time
Dad has allowed himself to show
himself or take off the mask in
many years. I feel good and con-
fident, so I leave Dad and turn
to the son. In all the transcript,
this nonverbal interaction was
probably far more important
than anything I said.

Shep: (To the son) How do you
feel when Mom nags you?

S: I feel angry. Why is
she always after me?
Other kids' mothers let
them stay out later
than 9 o'clock.

Although the son is being
trained not to grow up (the
opposite of Dad), the bottom
line is that he is being trained
to feel anger and despair (the
same as Dad).

Shep: (To Mom) How do you
feel when your son
doesn't wear warm
clothes or when he snif-
fles and coughs?

M: Scared.

Shep: Who were you scared of
when you were little?

M: My mother. I had to take
care of her. I had all the
responsibility.

Shep: How do you feel when
Dad doesn't help
discipline your son?

Edited Transcript of Family Interview	Comments

(I draw the following triangle on the blackboard as I talk to the family. Figure 7)

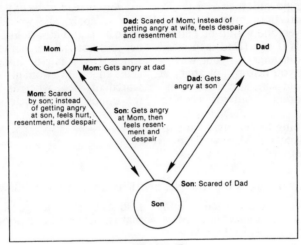

Figure 7
Victim-and-Feelings Triangle

M: I get angry at him.

Shep: (To Dad) Do you get angry at Mom when she nags your son?

F: No, I never got angry at my mother, either. I feel despair.

> Great! Dad is one step ahead of me; he is working through his own patterns! Dad is depressed and can't even feel anger at Mom/wife.

Shep: For a hunch, when your son get angry at Mom and calls her names, deep down a part of you feels good, that check out?

> I had a hunch that Dad was aware he was approving of his son's behavior, and checked it out. If Dad had said no, the issue would have been dropped.

F: Yes.

Shep: (To the son) You ever give Dad static?

S: No, he would knock my block off. He doesn't kid around.

Edited Transcript of Family Interview	Comments
Shep: So there it is (pointing to Figure 7).	
Shep: (Reads the feelings triangle and goes over it with the family.) Seems everyone would be better off if you (Dad) expressed your anger to your wife, if you (Mom) got angry at your son, and if (to both parents) your son weren't so scared of Dad. I'm going to get myself a cup of coffee. Meanwhile, mull over what's going on.	Of course, if Mom got angry at the son instead of feeling scared, hurt, despair, she would discipline him, and he would listen to her and not call her names. The son is Dad's mirror image and gets angry at women and is scared of men, whereas Dad is the opposite; nonetheless, both feel despair.

(The family discusses the triangle, and I return in a few minutes.)

F: We have discussed it, and there is a *good deal* of truth in everything you say.	Dad sees this as a "good deal;" that is, he's getting a good deal.
Shep: (To the family) I know you all want to be happy and (to the parents) you want your son to be happy. Something has to be done to break up the pattern.	
Shep: (To the son) What would you like from your father?	
S: (Quiet for a long time) I dunno.	"I dunno" means "I don't say no." Son is scared to ask from Dad.
Shep: Have much fun with Dad?	
S: Nah.	
Shep: What could you and Dad do together that would be fun for you?	
S: Go camping. We went last year all by ourselves (without Mom).	The son's voice is animated and happy. He wants to be close to Dad, Lord Mayor, and get away from Mom, Pied Piper.

Edited Transcript of Family Interview	Comments
Shep: That's in the summer. What could you do this coming week? (It's October).	
S: Go to a ballgame, but he has to work.	
Shep: What would you like from your mother?	
S: For her to stop nagging me and let me stay out later with the other kids and not ask me so many questions like what I did in school, what I ate for lunch.	
Shep: (To Mom) What would you like from Dad?	
M: I would like him to help me with our son and to listen to me when I talk to him, and be home more often, and to be home when he (the son) is home. All he does is watch television and sleep.	
Shep: What could you do together with Dad that would be fun?	
M: I like to go dancing. We haven't been dancing in years.	My hunch is that Mom and Dad don't have much of a sex life, but they are not here for couples counseling, and it is too early in therapy to raise the issue. Dancing is often a vertical expression of a horizontal desire.
Shep: (To Mom) Are you willing to let your son stay out until 10:30 with the other kids if he changes his behavior?	
M: Yes.	

Edited Transcript of Family Interview	Comments
Shep: (To Dad) I know both you and Mom want your son to be happy. Are you willing to take your son to a ballgame and spend time with him this coming week, and to take Mom to dinner and a dance if she lays off the kid? I know it will be hard on you, what with the time element and all the work you have to do.	Dad plays the martyred, silent type. The intervention here "it will be hard on you" is more likely to get Dad to take his son to a ballgame and his wife dancing than if I said, "I want you and your son and you and your wife to have fun together." As a technique, asking the parents to sacrifice themselves for the sake of the child, to hold hands, hug, have fun, go dancing, and the like, is highly effective if they are programmed to play martyr!
F: (Thinks for a while) Yes, I can arrange it. (Said with great finality)	Banzai!!

The pattern can be gone into from any part of the triangle. Contracts are now negotiated to break up the family patterns. Dad will take Mom dancing and Son to a ballgame. Mom will stop asking Son questions, will allow him to stay out till ten-thirty, and will not nag him. Instead, if she wants Son to do anything, she is to write it down and tell Dad, and Dad will tell Son (bringing Dad and Son closer together and Mom and Dad closer). Son will stop calling Mom names, be civil, and dress adequately. (The "dress adequately" is a bummer put in at Mom's insistence; her idea of adequate is a fur parka if the temperature drops below 62 degrees; Son's idea of adequate is a sweatshirt in subzero temperature; Dad couldn't care less.)

I tell the family, "I predict you will not have 100 percent success; after all, this situation has been going on a long time," and the family agree to return next week to report.

"I predict you will not have 100 percent success" gives the family the opportunity to prove I am wrong by being 100 percent successful. If they are not 100 percent successful, they will at least feel successful, because they were not expected to do "it all."

Moreover, if they are successful, Mom will be telling Dad

that Son isn't doing so and so, Dad will tell Son to do so and so, and Mom will be closer to Dad, and Dad will be closer to Son. I did not choose to have Son report to Dad if Mom nagged him, since Dad is in the business of telling Mom she "is too hard on the boy" anyway.

Within four months (eight sessions), Dad had decided to "raise his estimates" to his customers by 10 percent. Since he netted a 10 percent profit on his gross sale price, this meant he would either double his income or lose some customers. If he doubled his income, he could afford to hire more help and work fewer hours. If he lost some customers, he would still make as much as, if not more than, he made before the estimate increase, and would not have to work seventy hours a week.

After the family sessions, Dad spent more time with his wife; Mom and Dad joined a health club and agreed that once a week they would go dancing or to a local event. (Previously, when they did go out together, they would go to a movie, concert, or theater and be spectators instead of participants.)

Some of Mom's problems with her son disappeared. Those which remained didn't bother her so much as they did before our interview.

This case, I would say, is within "average" range, and change was relatively easy.

In psychotic families, however, where one of the parents is bound and determined to rescue the victim, change can be very difficult.

The victim, when he's down and out, is a pussycat, the nicest person you'd ever want to meet: Just bail me out of this mess. Save me from this scrape. Get me a car. Get me a job. Get me an apartment. Put me back in school—and this time it will be different. The rescuing parent will then come forth and take care of the child. The minute he or she does, there's a shift, and the child becomes vicious: How can I drive around in a two-year-old car? How can I get along at school on a paltry allowance of $800 a month?

No matter what the rescuer does, the child will manage to undo it. So if they pay for his trip to Florida, the child will decide he doesn't like it, or he will stay and become a beach bum. If they pay his tuition at school, he'll drop out. They'll get him an apartment in the city, and he'll hate his roommate. They'll give him an adequate allowance, and he won't be able to survive on normal foods and will have to go in for epicurean delights and then have his roommate eat them up so he can go broke and show up on his parents' doorstep for more "help." "This is the last time, if you'll only_____."

The clinical case of Leo, aged thirty-five, illustrates this process. Leo's father supported him financially while he was in college. However, Leo would spend his allowance on record albums and then steal food from the cafeteria. He looked like a wild man, unkempt, with a head of hair that stood straight out. He probably hadn't had a haircut in months. He also had a habit of stalking the girls' dorms and would scare the girls by staring at them. At one point, he was arrested and Dad bailed him out with the understanding that Leo would get free legal aid; however, when he reported that his weekly allowance was $200, he was told him he was ineligible for legal aid. The truth was that he received only $75 a week; as he explained later to Dad, "How would it look if I told them I received only $75 a week?" So, Dad came to the rescue and paid legal counsel, and Leo remained "helpless."

If the parent stops rescuing, the Victim will escalate and get into a blackmail game of "I'll kill myself." The only hope in such a system is to get the Rescuer to stop rescuing, and that can be very difficult. The Rescuer will take the child from psychiatrist to psychiatrist, from Freud to fraud, looking for some magic pill that can cure his poor, sick child. Meanwhile, the parents are unaware of their own contribution to the system.

In the case of the single-parent family, the remaining spouse will have a full set of parent messages in his or head and will fill the roles of both parents. Where both parents of young children die, whoever brings up the children becomes the parent figures and teaches the children the favorite bad feelings and games.

The following clinical case illustrates one of the few clients I referred out in a hurry. Although I am against medication in general and as a philosophical issue, since it keeps the Victim helpless and stops the client from working through, sometimes medication is absolutely imperative.

A widow with three children was referred to me by a school psychologist. She was having problems with the oldest, a fourteen-year-old son. She wanted to send him alone, but I insisted they come together. The father had died several years earlier. Getting the mother to come was a problem, since she was highly phobic and left the house only for bare necessities.

In our first interview, the child displayed prepsychotic behavior: He would leave the here and now; he had peculiar eye motions; he made peculiar gestures with his hands; he would raise his arms over his head, cross them around the back of his neck from the other side and scratch the side of his nose opposite to that of the hand—for example, he would scratch the left side of his nose with his right hand. He wanted to be "left alone." The interview follows.

Shep: What was life like when you were little?
Mom: I lived in a three-bedroom apartment in Brooklyn in a bad neighborhood, and my mother didn't let me out to play much.
Shep: How are you re-creating your early life?
Mom: Now I live in a good neighborhood in the suburbs in an eight-room house, but I never go out. I'm phobic.

I got a commitment from the mother to come to an introductory lecture, with the explanation that her attendance would help her change her son's behavior. If she liked the lecture, she would then join a group. My plan was to have her begin to get her needs for social contacts met in other ways than from her children. Since she "couldn't" drive as far as my office (about eight miles) alone, the son agreed to come with her.

Mom: (To Son) You agreed to come with me, but you're going to blackmail me.
Son: No, I won't.
Mom: (Whines) Yes, you will. You'll want something in return.
Son: No, leave me alone, all I want is for you to leave me alone.
Mom: I know you, you'll want to use the car, or something. You will blackmail me.

Son: (Now sounding angry and in despair) No, all I want is
            for you to leave me alone.

Mom: You have a terrible temper. Someday you'll come at
            me with a knife.

Shep: (To Mom) Hold it. I'm referring you to a psychiatrist.
            You never told me your son has this terrible temper.
            (To Son) She is impossible. Get her to the psychiatrist
            before she does get you to stick a knife in her.

The psychiatrist prescribed tranquilizers for Mom and then
worked with her through her phobia so she could go to his office alone. What was needed was separation, not togetherness.

Mom had structured her whole life around her children and
was destroying them in the process. When Mom began to
socialize and get her needs met elsewhere, her son's symptoms
disappeared.

Studying volumes on family therapy is not necessary. Once
you see the process, all the case are variations and repetitions.
Over the past few years, I have taught the material covered in
this chapter to groups of lay people. Many have reported that
they were able to problem-solve and see changes in their family
relationships. If you are interested in solving your family problems, I suggest you go over the chapter with your family and
devise solutions that are mutually agreeable and of benefit to
each and every member of the family.

Throughout this book, I have described elements or facets
of a process, each facet being simple and easy to understand.
Even so, I would like to end the book with the following appropriate quotation.

It is only as the result of century long labours of the wisest of
men that anything much has been discovered, and that as a
result of countless false starts and mistakes . . . The fact
that the regions of nature actually covered by known laws
are few and fragmentary is concealed by the natural tendency to crowd our experience into those particular regions . . .
we seek out those parts which are unknown and familiar and
avoid those that are unknown and unfamiliar . . . That our
knowledge only illuminates a small corner of the Universe,

that it is incomplete, approximate, tentative and merely probable need not disconcert us.*

Be my guest, help yourself, and thank you for reading my book.

*A.D. Richte, *Scientific Method*, Harcourt Brace Jovanovich, New York, 1923, pp. 201—202.

Epilogue

No one has a contract with God, yet many act as if they do, as if they will live forever, leading lives of quiet desperation, *waiting* for their spouse to change, *hoping* things will get better, and in the process role-modeling misery and self-inconsideration, passing on unhappiness to their children.

WHAT PLEASURE WE DERIVE
UPON THIS OVERCROWDED EARTH
IN MAKING AND REMAKING
OUR OWN IMAGE
WHEN ANY FOOL COULD TELL US
WHERE THE GIFT OF LIFE'S CONCERNED
WE TAKE FOR GRANTED
WHAT SHOULD BE A PRIVILEGE

THE CHILDREN OF THE WORLD
ARE DOOMED
BEFORE THEY REACH A SCHOOL
BY FAM'LIES WHO ARE UNPREPARED
AND CARELESS
AS LONG AS PROCREATION
IS A PARADISE FOR FOOLS
THE WORLD WILL BE THE VICTIM
OF ITS PARENTS

TEACH THE CHILDREN OF THE WORLD
TEACH THEM NOW BEFORE IT GETS TOO LATE
TEACH THEM HOW TO BE THE PARENTS
OF TOMORROW
OR THEY'LL BECOME THE PARENTS OF TODAY
AND PASS ON ALL OUR HATE AND MADNESS
TO A WHOLE NEW GENERATION
AND SO IT GOES AD INFINITUM
AD NAUSEUM
AMEN . . .

Anthony Newley